Imagine You Only Had One
Life

What Would You Do With It?

Imagine You Only Had One Life

What Would You Do With It?

A guide to figuring out what you really want to do with your life and directions on how to actually make it happen

by

Paul Green

Contents

Preamble

"Imagine you only had one life. What would you do with it?" – Doesn't that strike you as a rather odd question, as a very odd thing to say?

Let's face it most people actually know or believe that they do in fact only have one life and if they mess it up they don't get a second chance. But that is not how a lot of us tend to actually live our lives. Many of us just let the weeks, months and years drift on as if we had an infinite amount of time; putting our dreams on the 'to-do-later' peg. Dreams which gradually gather dust and rarely get revisited. But then occasionally we get a rude awakening, a bit of a jolt, and think, "How did I get here? This is not where I expected to be. This is not what I wanted out of life." We seem to have sort of ended up where we are either by accident, or maybe we have been pushed by events outside of our control. This jolt of realisation might come from some form of major or minor life crisis. Sometimes it is simply a growing feeling of dissatisfaction with our lot, or maybe we are feeling stuck in a rut. This jolt can happen to all people at any stage of their lives. It is really very unpleasant to feel that we are leading a life that does not feel like it belongs to us. A bit like acting in a play

1

or film and being made to follow someone else's script; reading lines written by someone else.

This book is aimed at helping you to use this realisation that you want something else out of life and use it as the pivot point to get from where you are right now to the life you actually want. And, believe me, actually knowing what you want in the first place it is not easy. We will cover this aspect in a lot of detail.

This is possibly the only self-help book you will ever use. Hang on, "The only self-help book you will ever use" – That's possibly an even odder thing to say. Don't I mean, 'the only self-help book you will ever need'? That's what the marketing hype usually says. No, it's not a mistake. The word 'use' is very deliberate. There are many very good self-help books out there. But if you don't use them, they won't work. That is a simple self-evident truth. If you don't believe me, join a gym and then never use it; tell me how much fitter you become in 12 months' time – not much I'll warrant. The purpose of this book is to be used and not just read. The focus is on things that work and things that are useful and doable. Each section will introduce you to things for you to try. With a specific "9 things to do" at the end of the three main sections in Part One.

There might be many reasons you have picked up this book. And when I say 'picked up' I mean, read the first few free pages on Amazon, borrowed it from a friend, or found it in a second hand bookshop etc. Or you might have looked at the cover and thought it was a history of origami paper boats. It's not a history of origami boats by the way.

There are many reasons we are prompted to make changes in the way our lives are going. There might be a major (negative) change forced on us, the death of a loved one, relationship breakdown, redundancy, accident, or illness etc. Life can be full of surprises, some good some bad, and it does sometimes throw us a curved ball. Or there might be a positive surprise and opportunity for change, an inheritance, retirement, promotion, graduation etc. Or it might be fairly neutral. Maybe you have a choice to make. You are about to start or finish study, possibly the children have just left home and you have some free time and a spare room etc.

Or, as happens surprisingly quite often, you might be sitting on a beach somewhere wondering why we only get two weeks a year vacation in our 50 or so years of working life. "Is this really what I want to do with my life?" we ponder. Research regularly shows that at any one time up to 70% of people in work are either disengaged or dissatisfied with their current job or career choice. That statistic alone shows that there are many people who want to change at least something about the direction of their lives.

Whether you know, or think you know, what you want to do with your life, but don't know how to get there, or you don't even know where you are right now, or you haven't got a clue where you want to get to, or any combination of these; this book could well be for you. We will cover all this and more. And I really hope that you will find it "useful".

The three key sections in this book are in Part One, they are:

1. What do I want to do?
2. How do I get there?
3. Aphorisms and how to use them

Details of the content and purpose of these sections are covered in the Introduction which is coming up soon. Don't worry, it will all make sense in a few pages, and I will guide you through how to actually use this book. So for now just relax and read on.

Part Two consists of two 'bonus' chapters. They are very applicable to the tools and methods covered in Part One and have been added to augment the earlier content.

The first section in Part One is an example 'Life Audit'. This can be a useful exercise in figuring out 'where I am right now and how I got here'. It can also help to see how some of the techniques in this book can be applied to something you already know very well. Namely, your life up to this point. But we are getting ahead of ourselves a bit. This will all be introduced as we get going.

The second section in Part Two is all about Anxiety. I have worked a lot with people with Anxiety. It can be very debilitating. Anxiety makes us avoid doing things. And avoiding doing things makes anxiety worse. Which makes us avoid doing things. Which makes anxiety worse... You get the picture. It can be a horrible vicious cycle. Once we get caught in this cycle it starts to become the 'norm'. We become so used to avoiding any changes that we just drift on. We start to put more and more hopes and dreams onto our CANNOT list (Things we unquestionably believe we CANNOT do) – there will be more about the CANNOT list later. We then start to believe that change is impossible. If Anxiety dominates your life then it is highly unlikely that you will be able to lead the life you want. And even if you do not suffer from Anxiety to a debilitating level, it is worth knowing about as you almost certainly know someone who does. It might help the way you look at their experience of their life. And importantly, some of the mechanisms around Anxiety are major factors in Procrastination, and we might not even notice that these mechanisms are affecting us. Procrastination is simply putting things off until later. But of course, later never comes and we never move from where we are.

Procrastination is also covered throughout the first Part of the book as it is so key. Many of the techniques I will be introducing are designed to help you overcome this awful, but common, habit. I know very few people who are not afflicted by this. Procrastination makes us kick the can down the street and promise that we'll deal with it tomorrow. Unfortunately tomorrow never comes, and we end up never doing the things we need to do in order to get to where we want to go.

The ideas in this book have been developed from my experience over many years of working with people, individuals and families in various therapeutic and support roles. There are elements drawn from Solution-Focused Brief Therapy as well as CBT (Cognitive Behavioural Therapy) and other techniques such as Motivational Interviewing etc. I have also used some concepts drawn from working in the business environment including process analysis and project management as well as some basic principles from psychology and philosophy. Almost all are derived from a pretty solid base of 'what works' evidence and you certainly won't be introduced to any outlandish fantastical theories simply grabbed from thin air. I believe that the overall combination of the tools, techniques, methods and metaphors in this book, and the way they are presented, can be used by those reading it to move towards a more fulfilling 'preferred future'.

Anyway, that is enough of a preamble to set the scene. Let's have more of a detailed introduction and then get our heads down and get on with it.

Introduction

What is my aim in writing this book? Simple, I would like it to be "useful" for you. Gosh, useful? That doesn't seem like a very ambitious goal does it. Do I not want it to be the best self-help book ever, or something that will transform its readers' lives beyond all compare? Well if any of that happens I will be very happy indeed, of course I will. However, I do think that the word "useful" is a very important and underestimated one. Let's be honest, how many of us have bought the next best thing (abs developer, miracle kitchen gadget, one-spanner-fits-all etc) and a few days or weeks later it is left languishing in a drawer never to be used again. The next best thing is actually of no use at all if it isn't actually used. I recently watched a TV program where viewers were asked to send in photographs of exercise machines they had bought in the past to show how they were being used now. You've guessed it. Most were being used as some sort of clothes horse with laundry draped all over them. Now to some extent I suppose that they were at least being used for something. And maybe this book is just the right thickness to wedge under that table leg and stop it wobbling – although I don't recommend this if you have the Kindle version – That is definitely not the sort of "useful" I mean.

When I have conducted therapy sessions, I usually have someone booked in for the next few weeks; typically 6 to 10. I typically start off with a variation of the "useful" question. Quite often, but not always, people think they know why they have come. They sort of know what the problem (negatively) affecting their life might be, and they definitely want things to be better, but many (probably most) have not really thought beyond that.

The "useful" question in the therapy context is broadly as follows; "What needs to change over the course of this therapy for you to be able to look back and be able to say that it was useful coming along to see me?" This question then prompts a discussion on what a 'preferred future' for the individual (or family) might look like and what sort of changes, skills, techniques, approaches and new ways of managing and organising their lives might help to get them there. That is, what new ways of doing things can we "use" that will help us now and in the future that will get us to where we want to be and help us to not slip back into old ways?

The best tools in the world will not help us if it they are never used. As I have already commented, garages and sheds across the land are filled with excellent fitness machines that would probably all give the abs (abdominal muscles – that 6-pack look; you know the one) we desire. But only if they are used and found to be "useful" and useable. I am sure that many people do stick with it, and good for them. I don't want this book to be a 'good read' which the reader thinks could well help them get a lot more out of their life, but it then sits on the shelf gathering dust; or the Kindle equivalent of dust. I have tried to present the ideas in this book in such a way that you will use them, and keep coming back to them. I want you to use this book to consider what your 'preferred future' might be and then be able to use the techniques in it to help you move towards actually living that preferred future.

Now this is not really a therapy book. But the "useful" question is still... uhm... well, useful. The "useful" question for this book would be more along the lines of, "What needs to happen for you in the course of working through this book for you to be able to look back and say it was useful reading it?"

At this stage your answers might be quite vague, or possibly very specific. If you want, feel free to jot down some ideas or simply say a few things out loud and see how they look or sound. You can get back to these later once you have read through this book the first time. The first time? Yes, I am going to recommend that you read it twice, but more of that later. The chances are (unless you really did think this was a book about origami boats) that you are going through, or planning, some sort of transition; A change from one state of affairs to another. This could be major or minor, voluntary or forced. Let us have a look at some 'typical' things you might be hoping to get from reading through this book.

More general answers to the 'useful' question might be along the lines of:

- I would want to know what I really want from my life and how to get it.
- I want to understand the sort of changes I need to make to lead a more fulfilled life.
- I try and make New Year resolutions each year, but I always struggle to figure out what they should be, and I never stick to them anyway. I want that to change.

- I have never really known how to take control of my life and make decisions about where I wanted it to go. I want this book to show me how to do this
- A friend read this book and said it was useful for him/her, so I wanted to see if it would be useful for me.

More specific answers might be along the lines of:

- "I want to change career from being an accountant and start to work with animals. And I want to be able to put a plan together to do this".

  Career choice is a big one. Sometimes we take a job and then get stuck with it. We don't feel that it is a real career or a proper vocation. "It pays the rent/mortgage, but it's not me". We might be starting off with our first job, or may have been working for 20 years. Maybe you are thinking of starting your own business or re-training.
- "I want to be happy and healthy; I want to know how to do that".

  Being able to make a change in lifestyle to become healthier and happier is a big one. I worked as a gym instructor for a while and the phrase, "I'm fat, I'm forty, and I'm fed up", was pretty much the most common statement that people would say to me during the one-to-one induction process when I asked what they wanted to achieve. What they wanted was to become, "fit, forty and fabulous"

  By the way, the next most common statements were exactly the same, but substituting the words 'thirty', 'fifty', and 'sixty' into the above bullet points. And to be fair, people in their 20's and 70's were not too far adrift either.

Your answers may be completely different from any of the above. That is fine. It would be a very strange, and dare I say boring, world if we all wanted to get the same thing out of our lives; or even out of this book.

Am I a fan of self-help books? Well, they are not all good, and they are not all bad. If one works for you then that is surely good enough. Many seem to promise wealth and happiness beyond the dreams of avarice, and just take for granted that this is what we all want. I am most definitely a great fan of self-help as the way to make changes in our lives. Sometimes we all need a bit of coaching, but at the end of the day it is 'my life' that I want to change, and I firmly believe that the best coaches actually teach us how to become our own coach. I don't like to follow other people – I like to forge my own way. I'm not alone, I think most of us do. It's no coincidence that the most popular choice of music people want to be played at their funeral is Frank Sinatra singing 'My Way'. My Way is not necessarily the same as Your Way and it is really important to acknowledge this. I am not going to tell you what to do to get what I want you to get. What I am going to do is show you ways that you can figure out what you really want and then show you ways that will help you get to where you want to be. Does that sound useful? If it doesn't sound useful then we might have a problem, but if it does sound useful then read on.

I will try and use different examples, metaphors, analogies and aphorisms throughout to try and explain techniques you can use in different ways. Sometimes I will be a bit chatty and light hearted. That doesn't mean that I don't take this very seriously. I really do take it seriously. In fact, almost nothing saddens me more that to see someone living an unfulfilled life. And that is really the motivation for me writing this book. And if it helps some of you to move towards a more preferred future, even a little bit, then I will be very happy indeed.

So, how should you use this book? I would suggest that you read straight through Part One and Part Two without doing the suggested actions. But do feel free to do them if you want. This first time through will give you a solid understanding of the entire process and make it easier when you actually start to use the techniques. Once you have been round the first time you will be primed and ready to start back at page one but this time actually working through all of the suggestions and actions. Take some time over this; days, weeks or even months. Having a small, or large, notebook handy would be a good idea. Sometimes we get some great ideas that are worth capturing, but they can be fleeting unless we record them somehow. It is also good to have a record of your thought processes as they develop. Your thoughts might change as you work your way through. Indeed, your ideas and ambitions might also change as you start on the way to your new preferred future. No harm in that, but it is useful to keep track.

And if you already know that Anxiety might be a major factor for you, then flick straight to that section first and come back to the start after you have read it.

So, having said that I am not going to be prescriptive and simply tell you what you should be wanting out of your life we need to move on to the first substantial bit and work on that seemingly simple question that is actually very complex and difficult, namely;

What is it that I actually want to do with my life?

PART ONE

What do I want to do?

There is an old story, so pardon me if you have heard it. A young city business type is driving out into the countryside without his SatNav or any maps, and gets lost. He sees an older man leaning up against a gate contentedly chewing a piece of straw. The young driver stops and gets out of the car. "Excuse me, I'm lost, can you tell me how to get to Plumpton". The older man scrunches up his face deep in thought. His hands start to move left and right as he is mentally running through his options, scrunching up his face even more. After several moments he speaks, "Well, I'm afraid you can't get there if you start from here".

Of course we know that this is nonsense. We can get to anywhere from anywhere on the road network. However when it comes to our 'one life' it can sometimes, or often, feel that we can't. We can feel trapped in our lives and think that we have got ourselves into a position from which there is no possible route out. Or at least no route towards the preferred life that we actually want for ourselves. Often we don't even know where we are starting from. Our 'event horizon' is so restricted that we can't see beyond our immediate problems and constraints.

Our event horizon is how far we can see from where we are at the moment. If you were walking through a forest, your event horizon would not extend beyond a few feet. Literally not being able to see the wood for the trees. It would be very easy to get lost and wander around in circles. However, if you could get up in a helicopter you would have a much bigger perspective of the overall situation. I remember once when I was a child my parents took me to a large air show. The parking was not well organised (in a makeshift field) and when everyone tried to leave in their cars at the same time it became chaotic and gridlocked. The event horizon from inside the car was restricted to being able to see the next few vehicles surrounding us. I climbed a nearby tree and managed to get a very different perspective on the situation. I could see where the pinch points and bottlenecks were. I could also see a way out. I plotted a route in my head that would take us out of the main chaos and to the best exit. We were out in 20 minutes or so while the others, with their more restricted 'event horizon', were delayed for hours. The point being that to get to where we want, we sometimes have to extend our event horizon and gain a bigger perspective; to be able to see what might lie beyond what we can currently see. Another example might be that we are currently only just managing to make ends meet. We can just about make rent or pay the mortgage. Our (financial) event horizon does not go much further than the next pay cheque (pay check) and the pile of bills that need to be paid. Any ideas of planning to move home, getting a new job, or re-training for a different career do not even get a look in. However, in order to move on we need to try and see a bigger perspective that takes a much wide view of where we are, where we have been, and where we want to get to.

This is what we will cover next.

Where am I now?

So where should we try and start from? And how to we get to where we should start from? In fact, where are we right now? We need to consider all this before we start to decide where it is we want to get to. I don't know about you, but I almost always use my SatNav when I drive to somewhere new. 'SatNav' of course is short for Satellite Navigation. Satellites whirling around the earth (or are they standing still, I could never figure that one out) are basically only doing two things. They are very accurately allowing the small electronic device in our car to find out exactly where it is on planet earth and exactly what time it is – "You are {here} and the time is {now}". All the rest of the clever electronics, mapping software, computer code, voice synthesiser and algorithms are in the SatNav device itself. You 'tell' it where you want to go and it works out how to get you there (most of the time – although we probably all have our own SatNav horror stories). So let us take our event horizon right up to the satellite level and start to figure out where we think we are right now in our life. We already know that the time is 'now', but where are we in our lives? This is what we are going to look at first.

We are all at different stages of our lives – me writing this book and you reading it. We have probably all already gone through many different stages of life. Some good, some bad. We have possibly tried things that worked, and things that have failed. We might have felt that we were going in the right direction with our lives, only for something to change and we slip right back to where we started. It can sometimes seem that life is a bit like a game of snakes and ladders. We roll the dice. A random number moves us a number of steps along the board and if we are lucky we find a ladder and get a boost up the board, but if we are unlucky we find a snake and slip back down – sometimes right back to square one.

One of the things we will look at later is to do with actively choosing the metaphors we use to view our progress as we move towards what we want. Metaphors and Aphorisms (those short pithy little sayings about life) can be very powerful tools in helping us to really picture what we want and where we want to get to. Unfortunately negative metaphors are prone to jump into our heads automatically and stay there as we mull them over. These are sometimes called Negative Automatic Thoughts (NATs) and everyone gets them. The trick is to simply accept that they are there without fighting them and then calmly replace them with the thoughts and metaphors of our choosing. Positive metaphors need a pro-active push from us. There are very good reasons that the brain automatically hooks on to the negative thoughts, which will be covered later (particularly in the chapter on Anxiety in Part Two). However, it is not very useful (that word again) to have negative metaphors and images sloshing around in our heads. I would contend that the metaphor of a snakes and ladders board is not a good one. It is very demotivating to do a lot of work and then feel we have ended up 'right back where we started'. In fact, of course, we are not actually back where we started. We have, at the very least, amassed a lot of knowledge and experience on our journey which will stay with us.

So, where are we starting from? Well let's consider a well know model of that is used a lot with regard to behavioural change. 'Behavioural Change'? That sounds a bit formal doesn't it? All I mean by this is changing what we are currently doing in order to get to where we want to be. It may be that you read through this book and find out that you don't need to change what you are doing on a day-to-day basis too much in order to get to where you want to be. On the other hand, you might need to change quite a lot, or almost everything. Changing what we do (our behaviour) is almost always challenging, if not downright difficult. Getting stuck in our ways is exactly like being a small paper boat on a river that ends up wedged against the bank where the current took it. One model we can use to help us find out where we are right now is called the 'Stages of Change' model developed by Prochaska and DiClemente. You have almost certainly heard of this if you have ever tried to give up smoking or tried to lose weight. You might recognise the stages;

pre-contemplation
contemplation
preparation
action
maintenance
relapse.

The States of Change model is often drawn as a circle to show that we tend to go round this cycle a number of times in order to accomplish the change we want to make. For example, I gave up smoking about 25 years ago and must have been round this Stages of Change model five or six times before I finally put out my last cigarette.

However, this model is not without its critics and it does tend to be used as a framework for giving up negative, unhealthy or damaging behaviours rather than adopting positive ones. We will mainly be looking at the more positive side of the 'making a change' equation in this book; starting new and positive things in a pro-active way that are in line with what we want to get out of life.

So, anyway, to get back to the question; Where are we now? Where are we starting from? I am going to use the States of Change model headings as a way of figuring out where you might be in your life right now as you are reading this book. Have a read through the following and consider where you might be right now at the present time. By the way, I am not going to use the States of Change model as the way of figuring out what you want to do, or how to get there. It is simply a useful way of getting some perspective and orientation on where you are currently. It is a way that you can start to increase your event horizon. We will then figure out where you want to be and how you might go about getting there. So, let us have a walk through the different stage of the states of change model.

1 - Pre-contemplation

This is probably where most of us are most of the time. Jogging on from day to day in an OK manner. Just getting through the day is enough. This is my life – I'll just get on with it. I haven't even started to think about making any changes or seeking to change the direction of my life. Mind you, there must be a spark of something or you wouldn't have picked up this book, or downloaded it to your Kindle. So, you are very possibly not at this stage. Nevertheless, it is still worth thinking about this beginning stage of the process. We might be looking for change in one area, but not really noticing that actually there are a few other aspects of our lives that are meandering around aimlessly and could maybe do with a bit of a makeover.

"If you don't know where you are going, that is exactly where you will end up"

The above is an example of one of the Aphorisms (a short pithy statement) we will be looking at later. Don't worry too much about these aphorisms and metaphors at the moment. The ones I have picked out are deliberately designed to be a bit quirky and might have you furrowing your brow at first sight. They are chosen on purpose and the reason for the quirkiness will be explained later in the section on Aphorisms.

A lot of people probably live all of their lives contentedly just drifting along with the current. Have you ever played a game called Poohsticks? It comes from the Winnie the Pooh books by A A Milne. Basically two people stand one side of a bridge and throw a stick each into the river then run over to the other side and see which stick comes out first – that is the winner. By the way, this is a real game that people actually play and there is even a world championship.

Obviously which stick wins depends on the strength and direction of the current it finds itself in. Our lives can be seen a bit like something floating down a river from start to finish. I am going to use the metaphor of one of those origami paper boats; hence the picture on the cover of this book. The little paper boat just sort of keeps moving along wherever the drift takes it. Sometimes it gets stuck against a bank or obstruction and just stays there, sometimes it gets dashed against the rocks and eventually sinks, and sometimes it just randomly floats on at the total mercy of the current. An origami boat has no means of propulsion or steering. But we human beings do have both a means of steering and propulsion. We are more like a rowing boat in a river. We can choose to just drift with the current if we want – occasionally pushing ourselves off the bank with an oar when we get stuck, or we can proactively 'make way' and steer ourselves in the direction we want to go. Being proactive we can explore tributaries and lakes, stop off at places, or with a bit of effort row against the stream and take a 'missed' turning to get to where we want to be. This is not a perfect metaphor, but you get the gist. The pre-contemplation stage is the basic unconscious acceptance of simply drifting wherever the boat takes us without even realising that we have the means to change direction. We haven't really thought that there might be an alternative. As I said earlier, it is unlikely that you are at this stage; otherwise you wouldn't be reading this book. However, maybe there are elements of your life that you have not yet considered and with respect to those you are simply drifting along wherever the current takes you.

What do I mean by 'elements of your life'? These are the broad categories and areas of your life that are important and meaningful to you. Examples might be:

- Occupation. This could be paid work, unpaid work, career, study or anything similar
- Hobbies. Those things you like to devote time to when you get some spare time. These could be passive things like reading, cinema, or more active things like sports, travel or making things.
- Friends and people who matter. People you care about and like to be with. Husband/Wife, children, neighbours, etc.

- Helping others. Things I do that make me feel part of the community.
- Self-improvement. The development of practical or cognitive (intellectual, thinking, mental) skills. – learning to sew, knit, restore furniture, learn French, doing crosswords, reading history books etc
- Self-care. This could include healthy lifestyle (diet and exercise), physical and mental well-being, and also things like maintaining a healthy work-life balance.
- Spirituality and humanity. This could be based on your faith and religious beliefs, or ethics based principles such as vegetarianism or environmentalism etc.
- Creativity. Music, painting, acting, writing etc

That is not an extensive list, but might be enough to get you started in thinking about those different things in your life that are important to you; that have value for you.

Have a think about what the key areas or elements of your life might be. Are there things that you used to do and enjoy that you have drifted away from? Are there things that you are now doing that you have just drifted into? We will look at these questions more closely later.

2 - Contemplation

This is the thinking and pondering stage. However, it is not just empty thoughts and daydreaming; we even do daydreaming at the pre-contemplation stage. There is also a difference between being realistic or reaching for the stars, but both are allowed at this stage. At this stage we know that if we do decide to do something it will involve putting thoughts into action. It will mean making changes. Maybe small changes, maybe massive ones. But we will have to start steering our little origami boat rather than just letting it drift, and that means decisions must be made, plans must be formulated and action must be taken. But for the time being we are allowed to just think about things and ponder on how our life could be different.

We might be having thoughts along the following lines;

"Surely there must be something better than this."

"Is this all there is to my life?"

"How did I end up here anyway?"

"This is not where I wanted to be."

"How did 'they' (the people with the greener grass next door) get where they are? – that's where I want to be."

"I'm stuck and I don't have a clue what to do about it."

"I know there is a problem, but I'm not sure if there is anything I can do about it."

This is quite an uncomfortable stage. We sort of know that we want something different. We also feel that we could probably make some changes to get somewhere different. But we are not really sure exactly what it is we want, or even how to figure that out. Let alone how to actually make the changes and get it. And in any case, have I left it too late? Am I too old to be contemplating stuff like this? Am I too young to be contemplating stuff like this? Is the timing right? Will the timing ever be right?

This is a major thinking stage. We sit and ponder. Along the lines of, "I don't fully know what I want and I am not really sure what to do next, but I am going to think about it and explore my options. " Unfortunately our head is often full of more negative thoughts along the lines of, "if only such and such had happened (or hadn't happened)" –

my life would be so much better. Or the impossible pipe dreams of, "what if..." (often followed by "I won the lottery" - although we know deep down that this is not going to happen). It is really easy to give up at this stage as it just seems such an impossible task to change things. This is also a stage where those Negative Automatic Thoughts flood into our heads. We simply accept that we CANNOT change things. We have a CANNOT list hidden away somewhere that is so deeply embedded in our brain that we mostly don't even look at it any more. Each time we think of how we would like our lives to change a massive negative thought slams into our thought process and stops us even contemplating that it could become a reality. A bit like the earlier story about the chap wanting to get to Plumpton, we persuade ourselves that we can't actually get anywhere from where we are now. Sometimes we just put things off and wait for things to be different. We keep just drifting down the river wherever the current wants to take us. Might this be where you are right now?

The big trick here is to try and not hold ourselves back before we have even started. But remember, all we are doing at this stage is simply window shopping into a new preferred future. And there are no limits at this stage as to which windows we can peer into. We are actually allowed to completely ignore the CANNOT list at this point. Everything is possible.

I definitely believe that figuring out where we want to be (where we want to get to) is possibly the hardest part of the whole process. It is probably also the most important which is why we are going to explore it fully and in some detail. Let us just imagine for a moment that you had genuinely won a competition for a one week holiday of a lifetime – you are allowed to go anywhere on the planet, whatever the cost. How would you decide where to go? Some people might already have a particular destination in mind that they have always wanted to visit. Others might want to revisit a place they had been before that holds cherished memories. Have a go at this. Jot some ideas down in a notebook. I don't know about you, but I am struggling to tie down one (and I am only allowed one) I would really go for. I can think of about 4 or 5 different places straight off; Caribbean Islands, remote Scottish mountains, unspoiled atolls in the Pacific, the bustle of city life in New York (or Paris, or London etc), A health spa in the Swiss mountains, an animal safari in Africa... What if I make the wrong choice and I speak to a fellow competition winner who went to a place I had never even heard of, but now I have heard of it, it sounds better than my choice? How do I choose a holiday destination and feel confident that I haven't chosen wrong? What if I use up my one chance and I don't enjoy it? What a wasted opportunity. I would be kicking myself for the rest of my life.

You might have heard of buyer's remorse. We spend ages saving up for, and choosing, something. Then when we actually have it, we start to fill our heads with doubts. Should I have bought it? Is it the right one? Have I wasted my money? If I had waited a month I could have bought it cheaper, or got the next model etc?

And that is how difficult it is to choose a free holiday, let alone one that you actually have to pay for. Choosing what to do with our lives is a lot more difficult. And if you imagine you only have one life, then it is even more difficult still.

"Imagine you only had one life, what would you do with it?"

This is a deliberately strangely worded question, and of course the title of this book. It is designed to take you out of your comfort zone and give your brain a bit of a jolt. When we know something so well that it becomes internalised, we no longer think about it as being of vital importance. We know that we only have one life and have internalised that fact, so we don't really think about what it means anymore. And because we don't think about it, we don't take it into consideration. Of course some people do experience a major life shock that focuses them on their mortality. This might be a lucky escape from an accident, a life limiting diagnosis, or the realisation that something that just happened to a friend could easily also happen to them. Very often people in such positions start to make very positive and deliberate decisions about what they want from their 'one life', which has all of a sudden become so much more precarious and therefore precious to them.

Take this example of another quirky question, "Imagine there was this thing called gravity that held us firmly on the ground, and stopped us flying into space; what would it be like?" Well in our daily lives we move about on the surface of the earth not worrying too much about 'sticking' to the ground or flying into space. We have experienced gravity since the day we were born and we take it for granted. It is completely internalised and we don't even think about it. But sometimes gravity does become important for us; falling off a ladder, tripping over a step, avoiding some falling masonry. And, if the legend is correct, even the great scientist Sir Isaac Newton took gravity for granted until he sat under a tree one day and an apple fell on his head. He didn't invent it, he simply noticed its existence and started to explore it in a way that no-one had before.

Now, I am not being morbid and trying to remind us that we are all mortal and are going to die some day. Whilst this is true it simply leads us to drawing up bucket lists and trying to cram in as many things as we can. Like filling our plates as much as possible before the 'all you can eat' buffet closes. Let's look at the question a different way. Firstly, imagine that you had as many lives as you wanted; an infinite number. You are now free to do with each one as you chose. You can be a train driver in one, a brain surgeon in another, devote your time to rescuing stray dogs in the third, and lie in bed all day eating chocolate and watching daytime TV in a fourth. You could even, and this is radical, and I don't recommend it, simply let your life drift along, like an origami boat in a stream and see where it takes you in a fifth. I suppose that if you really did have as many lives as you wanted then you could take this last option, and one of your lives would turn out just fine by the simple laws of chance and statistics. A bit like an infinite number of monkeys typing away at an infinite number of typewriters (a sort of mechanical word processor for younger readers). Statistics tells us that they would eventually produce the complete works of Shakespeare. So statistically, if we had an infinite number of lives we would eventually drift along the path of the one we really wanted.

But let's imagine that you don't have as many lives as you want. In fact you only have one. Is the last option the one you would really choose? Would you really want to just drift along rudderless like an origami boat in a stream? So, if that is not an option and you really did only have one life, what would you actually do with it?

It seems like we could spend a whole lifetime just trying to answer this single question.

"Imagine you only had one life, what would you do with it?"

I said earlier that I thought that this was the most difficult part of the process. But don't worry, we are going to spend quite some time on how to examine and answer this question.

This 'contemplation' stage is also a good stage to ponder the alternative ways we might get to where we want to be. The 'how-to-get-there' part is actually simpler than figuring out where we want to be, but it seems much harder as we know it will actually mean doing something. And doing something will inevitably mean doing something different from what we are doing now; and it will also mean doing something different for an extended period until we get to where we wanted to be. – And even then we will probably still be doing things we are not doing now. That can feel intimidating, particularly if we are not used to making changes, or have low self-belief in our own ability to make changes. We may never have steered our own lives before, and that can seem like a big and daunting task. Anxiety and Procrastination can kick in big time here. They are covered in the second section of Part Two.

So, so for the sake of argument, let us just imagine for the moment that we have answered the question. We know what we want out of life and we have some idea of how we might get there. As you read this, you might even consider that you are already at this stage and are bursting to get on and make it happen. However, I would still advise going through the rest of this section of this book where we will really work through this key question. In the meantime let us have a look at the next step on the States of Change model.

3 - Preparation

This is the final stage before we actually start to make the changes happen. This is also the final decision stage before we actually make the 'jump' and do it. This can be a scary stage. It is a bit like standing on the top diving board and looking down. We have two main choices; we either jump, or slowly climb the stairs back down to the water level. We might become anxious about what we are about to do. Because Anxiety is such an important and debilitating thing, I have included a separate section in Part Two specifically on this horrible but entirely natural and understandable thing called Anxiety. I have treated a lot of people with Anxiety problems in my therapy sessions over the years. The good news is that Anxiety can be overcome and managed. So feel free to take a diversion and head straight for that part of the book if this is something of particular interest to you – but do come back. Otherwise, let's carry on.

So at this stage in the change cycle I am standing on the verge of doing something. I know I really want to make a change. I know what I want. I know where I want to get to. And I believe it will be worth it. I'm going to figure things out, make some plans, and then actually do something. I feel I'm ready for this and I'm willing to put some effort into doing something about it. This is the serious planning stage. We are not window shopping any more. We are actually intending to go into the shop and buy something.

I would recommend that this is a good point to do a bit of a Life Audit. I say 'bit of a' as if it was a simple thing. It really isn't. It is an honest look at how you got to where you are now. And importantly, the sort of choices and approaches you took as you were getting here. If done in an objective and honest way it can help to identify any specific strengths and weaknesses you have. Of course, if done in a negative and self-critical way it can be very de-motivating. Doing it in a negative way will not help you at all. We will cover how to avoid this.

There is an example Life Audit in Part Two. I use my own life as an example. I pondered about whether I should do this or just make something up, but then thought that I should step up to the mark and do myself exactly what I am asking you to do. Doing an Audit helps to get some perspective on your life and is a good way of practicing some of the suggestions in this book before you actually start doing them in reality to move towards your preferred future. There are plenty of questions that are asked and answered in the audit. Did I just drift? Was I making positive choices and changes? Were there good things that happened and helped me? Were there negative things that happened and have set me back, or even put me off ever trying again? Don't do a Life Audit right now. Read through the rest of Part One of this book and then get back to it. I will prompt you with a few actions and steps to take, so don't get too hung up with trying to remember what was said in an earlier part of the book. As I say, I also provide a Life Audit example audit later on in Part Two so you can see what one might look like. Plus, when you do get to the point of doing an audit it is important to do it against the backdrop of the techniques, tools, recommendations and aphorisms detailed in these pages. So it really helps to have read through all of Part One first.

4 - Action

This for many people is the main element. This can also feel like the most difficult part of the whole process. It can also be the most rewarding. It is where having a good plan really pays off. The ideas in our head get translated to real actions in the real world. With a good plan we know what we need to do each day. And the "day" really is the most important unit of time as we shall see later.

This is where the rubber hits the road. I'm walking the talk. Words into Action. Pattern changing. Out of my comfort zone. Taking the path less travelled. Living the dream? Not quite yet – but definitely 'doing', and not just daydreaming.

This stage is all about changing behaviour and actually doing something in the real world. I have mentioned CBT (Cognitive Behaviour Therapy) a few times before. Importantly, this is not a therapy book. However, some of the basic principles of CBT are valid in this stage. I have included some details on what CBT is and how it works under the section on Anxiety. I have worked as a CBT therapist for many years prior to writing this book. It is often referred to as a "talking therapy" and has been shown to be very successful in treating a variety of Anxiety disorders as well as Depression and a number of other problems. CBT shows how for any given situation there is a very real link between our thoughts (or cognitions) how we feel emotionally (our mood), how we feel physically and what we do (our behaviour, or actions). If any one of these elements changes, so do the others. The two that we can have most control over are our thoughts and our actions. In my experience CBT works best when both thoughts and actions are addressed. But what really makes a difference to the person in therapy is when their behaviour changes, when what they do changes, as this both helps them put their 'new' thinking into action and also changes their relationship with the world. So, I tend to refer to CBT as being as much of a "doing therapy" as a "talking therapy".

Possibly you were already at this Action stage at the point you picked up this book and were starting to feel a bit overwhelmed. Maybe you are thinking that your goal is unrealistic or unreachable. Maybe you have fallen into that trap that most of us do of – "Ready, Fire, Aim" rather than "Ready, Aim, Fire". If you feel you are starting from here I would suggest that you hit the pause button and read through the rest of Part One which will help you get the Ready and Aim parts sorted out before you move on to the part where you actually 'Fire' and take action to make it all happen.

5 - Maintenance

Maintaining our new preferred future life is not like being on autopilot. We are getting to where we want to be, or we are already there. But we still need to steer our little paper boat and watch for unwanted drift. It is always possible that we hit an unpredicted current which sweeps us off our course. These currents can be sudden or quite subtle so that we don't even notice them until we are well off course. Also, we can't control everything, so we need to be on the lookout for turbulent waters and unexpected obstacles. This is the point where it is important to review all of the previous stages and include a regular watch to monitor progress. Sometimes we use the word 'maintenance' to mean fixing something when it goes wrong. Many years ago when I was working as a Systems Engineer with computers (devices that that now seem positively prehistoric by today's standards). I was introduced to the term 'preventative maintenance'. This means looking out for things that typically can go wrong and fixing them before they do. A bit like giving our car a regular service and replacing the fan belt before it actually breaks and causes bigger problems. This stage is as much about predicting and preventing problems to keep our plans on track as it is about maintaining our original direction.

So at this maintenance stage we are well into implementing our plan. We are in action mode and seeing progress. It is working, but so am I - hard. I'm probably feeling more comfortable, getting used to this new way. Wow, this is working. It usually takes at least 6 weeks after you have reached your goal to get to the point of feeling comfortable with doing things differently. I am still able to look back and see that this is a better way. This is a really good time to check if we aren't in the pre-contemplation stage for other potential changes. An important point here is that all the different stages are not just a circle that goes round and round. We might be at several different stages at any one time for the different elements of our life.

6 - Relapse

I don't mean to be negative, and I am all about the positive. But things can, and do, go wrong. And when they do, we tend to revert back to a place we used to know – our old way of thinking, our old way of doing. This is when that Negative Automatic Thought, "I'm right back to square one" comes into our head.

Self-doubt creeps, or floods, in – "I knew I couldn't keep it going". "This is the real me". "I've failed". No this is not true; these are 'just' thoughts. Thoughts should be viewed as opinions, they are not facts. They can be very negative and destructive opinions. Again, have a look at the chapter on Anxiety in Part Two for an explanation of why our brain thinks it is protecting us by holding on to these negative thoughts.

Relapse is a natural stage in any change. In case of 'crisis' we almost always go back to the original way of doing things. But it is not back to square one. It is just a temporary sojourn off the rails to one side. We need to pre-prepare for relapse. At the very least we need to acknowledge that it is a natural part of any change process, so we shouldn't be surprised or upset when it happens. It most probably will happen at some point. And if it doesn't then fine – no harm in being prepared. A combination of using some powerful Aphorisms (the last chapter of Part One) and reviewing our previous strategies are key here. We tend to lose our sense of perspective when things go wrong. Our event horizon becomes more restricted and we lose the wider and longer term perspective. But put bluntly; if what we did before was working before, then it can and will work again.

Maybe this is the stage you feel you are at right now. Maybe you are at one of the other stages. Very possibly you recognise elements of all these stages from different parts of your life in the past. Whatever stage you are at, we are going to start marshalling our thoughts, plans and actions and work through things in a practical and methodological way to start getting this little drifting bobbing origami boat (our one and only life) under our control and start to steer it towards a destination of our choice. Our preferred future. Your preferred future.

Let's get going.

Making sure what I want to do fits with who I am

What do I want to do? Sounds like the easiest of all easy questions. Surely we daydream about what we want to do all the time. But it is not actually an easy question at all as we shall find out. And we will spend some time looking at how to approach answering it. But first, let me ask you what we really do consider to be an easy question.

"If you won the lottery what would you do?"

That's an easy question and possibly one that most people have thought about; even people who don't actually play the lottery. Buy a house – bigger house. Buy a car – bigger car. Go on a world cruise. Book up a place to take the first passenger flight to the moon. Give money to my family and friends…etc. In fact most people who really do win the lottery, certainly in the UK and USA, and probably elsewhere, do pretty much most of the above. A surprising number of people simply spend uncontrollably and lose the lot. Up to 30% of big money winners eventually declare bankruptcy. One or two have recklessly gambled their winnings away. Famously, Vivian Nicholson won £152,300 (about £3M or $3M give or take in today's money) on the UK Football Pools in 1961. When the papers asked what she was going to do with her winnings, she simply said, "spend, spend, spend!" And that is exactly what she did for three years until it all ran out.

A lot of research has been done on that vexing question as to whether winning the lottery actually makes us happier. The good news is that winning a large amount of money can actually increase overall life satisfaction (including long term financial security), the bad news is that it does not necessarily actually make you happier (our day to day mental state). Those who do achieve happiness after winning the lottery are found to be those whose spending is closely aligned to their life values. – So, if you are reading this book after having just won the lottery, please read on as it is aimed as much at you as it is at the rest of us who can sometimes struggle a bit to make financial ends meet. Not having enough money to meet the bills on a month by month basis can certainly cause misery and I will cover more on this later.

So, in a similar vein, if someone asks us what we want (in terms of our preferred future), some typical answers might be;

- To lose weight
- To be fitter
- To have more time for myself
- To have a good relationship
- To have more time with my children
- To give up smoking
- To win the lottery
- To pay off the mortgage
- To earn more money
- To work less
- To speak a foreign language
- To play a musical instrument
- To be able to paint/draw
- To be happy
- To retire

- To live in a warm country
- To have children
- To find a loving partner
- Etc – This list could go on forever

But, and here is the rub, if these are not aligned to our life values (to who we really are), we might well not end up any happier even if we manage to achieve these things. A bit like the imaginary lottery winner we considered just now.

So, here we go, let's have a look at the real question posed as the title of this book; "Imagine I only had one life, what would I do with it?"

Partly this is not an easy question, because at the root of it are the two fundamental questions that philosophers and others have been grappling with for hundreds if not thousands of years, namely:

1. What is the secret of life?
2. What is the meaning of life?

This is a practical book, not a philosophical one – although I do have a university degree in philosophy. So let's just answer these two questions straight off and get them out of the way. You might disagree, and that is fine as philosophers have been debating these questions for many hundreds of years. But the answers I have given below are ones that are actually useful and fit in with the approach I am putting forward in this book. And remember, this book is all about being "useful".

The answer to the first question, "What is the secret of life?" is simple. The secret of life is to only concern yourself with those things that you can do something about. Wow, that was easy, or was it? What this means is that there are things in our life that we can have some control or influence over, and other things that we have no control or influence over. Spending time worrying about things we can have no influence over is by definition a waste of time. More importantly, it is wasting time that could be better spent doing something else. And that 'something else' is of course working towards getting the life we want. It can be useful to have a bit of a clean out and consider those things that we are concerning ourselves with (thinking about, worrying about). Should some of them possiblybe confined to a (real) CANNOT list? These are the things that we should set aside and not waste our time on.

However, there is a big trap here, so be very careful. We also sometimes (often?) put things onto a CANNOT list of things when they shouldn't be there at all. For example, it would be wrong for me to put something onto the CANNOT list simply because it is a skill I would have to acquire and I have never actually properly tried to acquire it. One example of this could be the ability to learn a foreign language. I always thought I couldn't learn languages, and I had proof. After several years of learning French at school, I still couldn't speak French. Being able to speak a foreign language was put into my CANNOT pile. However, many years later I started to visit Germany and then had the opportunity to live there for a while. I learnt some German before I went, and continued to learn when I got there. To my great surprise, I learned enough to study for a Semester at Hamburg University. 'Learning a foreign language' is now off my CANNOT list. I still struggle, and I don't pick up languages as quickly or easily as some people I know – but it is possible. This gave me the confidence to spend eight months in Romania in 2011 doing voluntary work. I took 'learning a foreign language' off my CANNOT list and managed to learn enough Romanian to get by. Another big source of candidates for the CANNOT list is other people telling us that we cannot do something. Has that ever happened to you? I can't actually think of anyone I know who hasn't been told that they cannot (in the sense of are not able to) do something. There is quite an easy test to see if something really belongs on the CANNOT list. Simply ask yourself if the thing on your list is something other people can do. If they can, then so can you – most probably. Figure out what you need to do to make it happen and give it a go. But we are getting a bit ahead of ourselves.

And as for the second question "What is the meaning of life?" The answer is, "to actively seek out a life that is my authentic life". Whoa there, hang on, what? OK I admit it, this one is a bit philosophical, so let's try and make it more practical; more useable and useful. Let's break this down. "My authentic life" simply means a life that is progressing in line with my values; all the things that are true to who I am, what I believe in, what I like, how I like to be, and in accord with what is important and meaningful to me. "To actively seek out an authentic life" means to actually do what it takes to make sure that my life does progress in an authentic way. And if I do manage to do this I am conducting my life it in such a way that I am being true to myself – to who I really am. Is this still a bit up there in philosophical cloud land? Let's have a closer look at this in very practical terms as it is key in helping us answer that complex and difficult question of what to do with our 'one life'.

Here is something to do. Consider and list those things that are important to you. You might have started this earlier when we talked about the different elements of your life in the Pre-contemplation stage of the States of Change model. This will take quite a bit of thinking about and you might want to come back to the list over several days. You can either start to do this now, the first time you are reading through this section, or do it the second time through the book. It will make more sense the second time around, so that is what I recommend. The things you list are the things that fit comfortably with who you are and what you value. You might find it easier to fit these into different categories and even rank how important they are out of 10. So,"0/10" means, not at all important to me, I don't need this in my life at all, I don't get any sense of achievement or enjoyment doing this. "10/10" means, this is vital for my happiness and well-being, it is something I need in my life for it to be complete, I get a great sense of achievement or enjoyment from doing this. Do this for everything you can think of, not just the things you are actually doing at the moment. Include things that you used to do, and things that you used to want to do.

This exercise is easier if you think about possible categories and list everything you think of as important in that category. Here are some typical categories copied from the earlier section (I thought I would save you the hassle of referencing back to the previous section), but feel free to add more:

- Occupation. This could be paid work, unpaid work, career, study or anything similar
- Hobbies. Those things you like to devote time to when you get some spare time. These could be passive things like reading, cinema, or more active things like sports, travel or making things.

- Friends and people who matter. People you care about and like to be with. Husband/Wife, children, neighbours, etc.
- Helping others. Things I do that make me feel part of the community.
- Self-improvement. The development of practical or cognitive (intellectual, thinking, mental) skills. – learning to sew, knit, restore furniture, learn French, doing crosswords, reading history books etc
- Self-care. This could include healthy lifestyle (diet and exercise), physical and mental well-being, and also things like maintaining a healthy work-life balance.
- Spirituality and humanity. This could be based on your faith and religious beliefs, or ethics based principles such as vegetarianism or environmentalism etc.
- Creativity. Music, painting, acting, writing etc

Now consider and list those things you are actually doing in your life. Hopefully there will be some overlap with the first list. Maybe there won't. You might even find things that completely contradict each other. Here is a made-up example of a couple of lists. I have made them quite short for the purpose of illustration. You can make them as long or short as you wish:

List of things I value and add meaning to my life
- Being my own boss
- Working with people
- Working with Animals
- Reading historical novels
- Walking in the countryside
- Seeing friends

- Spending quality time with the children
- Learning to cook world cuisine
- Helping in the local community
- Playing the piano to a good standard so I can sing along with friends and family

Remember that some of these are things that that are meaningful and have value for you when you actually do them. Some might be things that have been on your wish list for some time and you have never somehow got round to them. Take the last one on the list. I used to joke that as a family we often stood around the piano at Christmas – wishing one of us could play it. Things on your wish list might be things that you wanted in the past, but have almost given up on. If they are valuable and meaningful for you, then put them in your 'things I value' list.

Things I am actually doing
- Working in an office under four layers of management
- Commuting three hours every day to get to the office
- Doing screen based work processing numbers and budgets
- Flopping down in front of the TV most evenings too exhausted to do anything else
- Taking the children to their sports clubs every Saturday morning
- Part of the local town committee organising the annual carnival
- Going to night school to learn Information Technology skills

- Contacting friends over social media
- Walking/camping holiday once a year

Compare your two lists. If they are pretty much the same, then you are already leading a life that is authentic to who you are – you are possibly quite content or even happy. That is a great place to start from. If the two lists are widely different then you are not really leading an authentic life, you are probably not content or happy. Things can change without us noticing. It is vital to re-draw and monitor these lists through every part of the process as you decide, plan and journey towards your preferred future.

You can see from the two made up lists above that there are many areas where there is a big gap between what I value and what I am doing – staring at a screen all day is not working with either people or animals, nor is working many layers down in a hierarchy even close to being my own boss. However, there are a few areas that are either close or pretty much matching – Helping organise the annual town carnival is certainly helping in the local community. There are a few which are also a bit questionable – is keeping in contact with friends only on social media really what I mean by 'seeing friends', and is one holiday a year walking in the countryside enough, or do I want to walk out of my front door and have the countryside right next to me to enjoy at any time? And what about the time spent commuting? Is that time wasted? Could that be better used learning to cook new world cuisine dishes or learning the piano, although possibly I might be able to spend this time reading historical novels if my commute was on a train or bus? And what about being a 'taxi driver' for the children's sports clubs at weekends. Is that really what I might mean by spending quality time with the children? You might also question why I am doing an evening course in Information Technology. This isn't related to any of my values at all. Possibly I am doing it to move up the ladder in my current job, but will that help me become my own boss? Possibly, possibly not. You can see that from even these two short (imaginary) lists we can have a sensible conversation with ourselves about what we are doing and why we are doing it. As noted earlier, not all of the things on your list will have the same importance or value to you. Putting a numerical value against the different items on the list can help to clarify just how important these values are in terms of figuring out what we want from our preferred future.

You can also go back to the first question about the secret of life (only concerning yourself with things you can do something about) and draw up what you believe to be your CANNOT list. You will probably find it difficult at first to come up with a CANNOT list as the things on it are buried so deep down that we rarely if ever even consider them. Or maybe you do think about them a lot, but only in terms of them being impossible. And of course there are some things that we spend time thinking about that really are impossible (turning back time being one that many people think about a lot). But have a go, be daring, and draw up as full a CANNOT list as possible. Then take a pen and put a line through only those things that you actually cannot have control over. Importantly, these must really be things that you cannot have influence over and not just things that you think you can't do. I find that putting a line through them is a good idea just in case they creep back and you start worrying about them again – you can still see them, but you are reminded that your task is to let them go and move on to thinking about something else. Remember that there is a fundamental difference between 'do not' and 'cannot'. Don't strike out the 'things I do not do' things on the list. If something has appeared on this CANNOT list, but it shouldn't be there and it is of value to you then put it on the list of things you value. For example it might be very important to me that I am my own boss and am working autonomously for myself. But I don't believe this is possible and I have put it on my CANNOT list. If at the moment I am working for someone else then I would not strike this through with a line as it is something I 'do not' do. But just because I am currently working for someone else does not mean that it cannot change. In fact changing this may be a key part of how I move towards my preferred future. So, 'being my own boss' really should be on the list of things that I value as it is important to me. So I should put, "being my own boss" on my values list.

However, imagine that what I really want is to be a world class football (and by football, I mean soccer – apologies to my American readers) player and this has been my dream since I was young and I am now in my 60's with a mobility problem. Then shouldn't I really consider it as something I 'cannot' do and therefore not even think about? Well, there are options available for all sports to be accessible for people of all ages and genders with all sorts of abilities and disabilities. So possibly being involved in football/soccer in whatever form is something that I would value, but it has been stuck on my CANNOT list and therefore I haven't even considered it as an option. But it should really go on my values list. Or maybe, the only joy I would get from football/soccer would be if I could compete at the highest level. In which case I should strike it through and move on – no more wasted time with me pondering 'what could have been'.

I am going to introduce a new metaphor here which I will refer to quite a lot in the rest of the book. I am going to refer to this metaphor as 'congruence' and am going to use a visual image of either hula hoops laying on the ground or circles drawn on paper. The word 'congruence' already has a meaning in both geometry and psychology. I am going to use the term in a different way that is related to these two, but is not quite the same. In psychology you would be considered to be congruent if your self-worth was aligned with your behaviours (what you do). In geometry it simply means two shapes that are the same size – although I am only going to consider the shape of a circle. In this book I am going to combine elements from both of these and use congruence to mean something very specific. I will explain.

Imagine you have two hula hoops of the same size. For younger readers, hula hoops are large plastic circular hoops (about 3 feet, 1 meter in diameter) which you rotate just about your hips and keep in motion by sort of rotating your hips. Seriously, it was a huge craze when I was younger and is almost impossible to describe. I also found it absolutely impossible to do – hula hooping is in my CANNOT list and I have never lost any sleep about that fact. So, take the two imaginary hula hoops and place them on the ground overlapping so that there is a bit of the ground contained by both hoops. Take your two lists of 'Things I value' and 'the things I actually do' and write them on imaginary pieces of paper along with the rating you gave them out of 10. Then sort these pieces of paper and place them in their respective places. The 'things I value' go in the left hula hoop. The things I actually do go into the right hand hula hoop. And the things that I both value and I actually do go into the centre portion – the shape made by the hoops overlapping. If you have nothing in the centre section, then you might as well move the two hula hoops apart so that they do not overlap. I would describe this situation as not being congruent, or being incongruent. If your 'things I actually do' hula hoop is full of things that are very different – or even opposed to things that have a high value for me, then move the hula hoops even further apart. For example, if being kind to animals was a 10/10 value for me and my job involved doing something that directly or indirectly caused animals pain, then this would be a very incongruent situation. However, if the middle section where the two hula hoops overlapped contained a lot of pieces of paper and there was not much in the two outer sections we could move the two hula hoops closed so that they were almost lying on top of each other. This would be a very congruent situation. There might be other scenarios. For example pieces of paper in the left and centre section and nothing in the right hand one. Or paper in the right and centre and nothing in the left section. All of the different scenarios give different levels of Congruence. The secret of life now becomes the task of changing what we do so that we can bring the two hula hoops into close alignment. And the secret of life (as I said before) is to live your authentic life which is the same as being congruent.

As you work your way through this book you will be asked to consider and monitor your congruence quite a lot. Also consider that in addition to what you start to change in 'what I do', you may also start to adjust and reappraise your values. Having the world's most exclusive collection of Faberge Tiaras (do Faberge make Tiaras?) might have been one of your key 10/10 values when you started the process. But after a few months of working as a volunteer in a kitten rescue centre (being kind to animals being another 10/10) you might decide that maybe just the one Diamante Tiara will do after all. Having a visual representation of your congruence is very valuable. I would encourage you to write lists, draw circles, and use colours. Doing this really increases your Event Horizon and helps you to see your way through the gridlocked car park; or down the river. You can use this concept of congruence as I have described it to test future possible options. Try this; take an imaginary career or profession that you quite fancy and have a go at seeing how congruent it might be for you. Is it more congruent than what you are currently doing, or less congruent? This is a really good way of ensuring that what you think you want from your one life really fits with who you are.

Have a look at the diagram below. I have taken just a small number of the items from the two lists from a few pages ago and written them into overlapping circles just to give an idea of what this might look like. It can be quite a powerful image to keep in our minds where we imagine

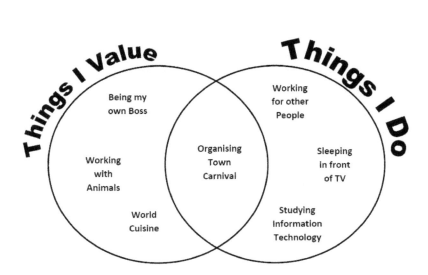

the circle of 'who I am' (my beliefs and values) to one side, and the circle of 'what I do' (my actual life as I live it) to the other side. The idea is to start to bring these two circles together so that they overlap and 'who I am' and 'what I do' pretty much occupy the same space.

A small number of you who managed to stay awake during math(s) class are probably thinking that I have just described drawing out a Venn diagram – and you would be right. Venn diagrams are a very good way showing in a very pictorial way when things (objects and qualities etc) of one class (a way of grouping things together based on some characteristic) also belong to another class. Venn diagrams are drawn as overlapping circles like our hula hoops. So why do I suggest the pictorial metaphor of imagining hula hoops rather than just drawing circles on paper. Well, mainly for both perspective and scale. We can imagine the hoops being yards/metres apart in a very incongruent situation. You might even suspect that your two hoops are miles apart in different valleys with a mountain in between as you are reading this. Also by viewing from above you can get a good perspective of the overall size and scope of where you are. You might want to scatter some of the items on your CANNOT list outside the hoops and decide whether they should really be in the CANNOT list or if you want to include them in your value hoop. The other thing you can do with movable hoops and movable pieces of paper is to start to play around with them a bit. Rearrange your 'what I value' and 'what I do' into what it would be like in your preferred future. Stand up and look at them. What does this feel like? Is this something worth going for? Is there anything missing? What might I need to change to get to this position? What help might I need from others to help me? Is that help available or forthcoming? Let me imagine putting the hula hoops of my loved one (or loved ones) next to mine. What is the overlap now? How might we work together to become more congruent as a couple (family, company, team etc). Most of this book is about you working out what you want to do with your life as an individual. However, the principles also apply if you are looking to include significant others.

I believe that this metaphor of congruence is a very powerful one. However, it will take practice. And as I said earlier, I would also strongly suggest that you do start to write out lists and also draw the circles on paper. Also, start to practice giving your congruence an overall score out of 10. Only you can decide what that number is, it is very subjective. A high score does not necessarily mean that everything is in both circles, but the important things almost certainly will be.

Visualising my preferred future as a possible reality

So here we go, this next part is absolutely key. You may have read the previous part about congruence once or even twice (if it the second time through this book). If it is your second time around it is really important that you do actually start to write things down and start to get a measure of both how congruent you are now, and how congruent you will be when you reach your new preferred future.

A very basic congruence check consists of checking how true the following two statements are:

- I believe in what I do
- I do what I believe in

If you can't give a 'yes true' answer to those then you are not living a congruent life. You are not being true to yourself. Get used to giving yourself a general number out of 10 as to how congruent you are feeling. Also, how would it feel to move just one congruence point up the scale? If you are currently 2/10, what would 3/10 feel like, how about 6/10? How much better would your life be?

We will now have a look at a few techniques to try and free our minds up and figure out what our preferred future might look like, and what we might want to do with our 'one life'. Unfortunately, particularly as we get older we start to shut, and even lock, a few doors in our minds and stick big notices on them saying, "Don't go in there!" It is actually quite difficult to really figure out what our values are, and just as difficult to admit that we might actually be doing something in our lives that we fundamentally disagree with in terms of how it really does not fit in with our values. We also become very good at justifying why something should remain in the CANNOT pile, and equally good at justifying why there are very good reasons why we are now doing something that deep down we would really want to reject and move away from. Now it could be that some of the things we might think of should indeed stay in the CANNOT pile, and conversely that some of the things we do that are not fully aligned with our values do have justifiable reasons as to why we continue to do them.

However, in order to start doing our congruency checks we need to start to learn how to move away from this editing mode that our brains are so good at. We do not want to veto or censor anything at this stage in our congruency investigation. Think about it, what is the worst that could happen? We might write something down and then cross it out at a later stage. But if we don't write it down in the first place we will prevent ourselves from even considering what could be a vital element in figuring out what we want to do in our one, and we do only have one, life. Also, if we reject something at the thought stage we could be falling into the trap of believing a Negative Automatic Thought (NAT). NATs are very powerful. We are programmed to believe them without any reflection at all. They are normally the result of inbuilt distorted and unreliable thinking processes that we are not even aware of. NATs are often (I would go as far as to say usually) at the root of most Anxiety and Depression disorders. They are that serious in impacting on our emotional happiness and wellbeing. So, we really need to be aware of their potential effect on our deliberations regarding investigating our possible congruent preferred future, and what we are going to do is gently put them to one side and ignore them.

One of the things that gets in the way of us even thinking about our true values and working towards making what we believe in become a possible reality is money. The need to survive financially is a real-world fact of life for the majority of us. I remember several years ago being very unhappy with both my job and career path (despite the fact that I was being paid quite well). I saw an advertisement for a dream job in a completely different field. The salary was about one third of what I was earning at the time. I didn't even apply although it would have taken my congruency score to about 9/10. What would the point have been? The new salary would have been less than the monthly mortgage let alone the rest of the bills, and there was also the need to actually put food on the table and eat. Plus, this was just as the housing market took a dive in the UK (late 1980's) and even selling the house and buying something smaller and cheaper wasn't an option as the house was worth a lot less than I had bought it for; and a lot less than what I still had to pay back. So, in a very real-world way I was stuck and there was no point in going for the new job. – So, shouldn't I just forget about this, lock it in one of the "Do not open!" rooms and fling it on the CANNOT pile, whilst also adding it as a NAT along the lines of, "Don't even think of doing something like that for a living, it's impossible"?

But something very important was going on here in respect of thinking about moving towards a congruent life which we will have a look at in a minute. Firstly let's consider "Happiness" as defined by Charles Dickens' character Mr Micawber in his 1850 novel David Copperfield, "Annual income twenty pounds, annual expenditure nineteen [pounds] nineteen [shillings] and six [pence], result happiness. Annual income twenty pounds, annual expenditure twenty pounds ought and six, result misery."

And I am not going to argue about that. Although I will (and did earlier) argue that money can't necessarily buy you happiness, I would also argue that not having enough money to pay your monthly bills will definitely bring you misery. So on our 'What are my Values' list we might have, "earning lots of money". However, based on the argument from Dickens above, we might think about this and modify it to "earning enough to pay my bills". And, if on the 'What am I actually doing' list we get to the point where "I earn enough to pay my bills"; then this would increase our congruence.

So going back to my earlier example, why would I have been so unhappy about not being able to apply for a job which, had I got it, would have meant I couldn't pay my bills? I had persuaded myself that this false dichotomy of, "either I can have the job I want or I can pay the bills, but not both", was true. If "having a job I love" is important for me and I score it highly and "I am working in a job I hate" is my reality then this is a very incongruent situation. I had firmly written "having a job I love" onto the CANNOT list. However, maybe the real issue here was that my monthly outgoings were too high and (despite the housing market problems) what was really needed was to downsize so that I both had enough to pay the (smaller) bills and do the job I loved. Now maybe I couldn't do that straight away, but if this was what I wanted in order to have a congruent and fulfilled life, then I could at least put together a plan to move in that direction.

Additionally, it may be that for some people, the work itself (what I actually do) is not so important for me. It may be more important to me to only work three days a week in a higher paying job that I don't particularly like in order that I can have more time and money to devote to the things I really do like. Maybe I work in some tough offshore job that keeps me away from home for 6 months in the year, but the 6 months that I have with the family are spent with them surfing on a Hawaiian island (obviously an extreme example). These are the sort of questions you can explore by playing about with your congruency (Venn) diagrams or lists.

I have said before that working out what we want to do with our lives is a more difficult step than we might initially think. We will meet the following Aphorism later in section three.

"Getting what you want is easy. Figuring out what you want is very difficult"

I have met a lot of people who get completely stuck at this step. I once spent a year trying to fill out a sheet of paper to describe my 'ideal life'. Don't get me wrong, I did other things in the meantime – but it is tricky.

Here are a few techniques and ideas. Try them all and have a good play around with them. If this is your second time of reading through then actually try them with a pen and paper (or felt pens and lots of paper!) to hand. Spend some time on them

Variation on the theme of The Miracle Question.

Sometimes we can be so mired down in thinking about the things that we don't like, the negative things in our lives, that it is almost impossible to paint any sort of picture of the 'preferred future' that we would like to live. We define everything in terms of getting rid of problems rather than moving towards solutions. So what is the issue with this? Surely it is useful to know what obstacles and problems we need to overcome in order to move forward. Unfortunately, sometimes when we only see problems in front of us we are actually building a wall out of distorted Negative Automatic Thoughts which we can't see through. And what is worse, they are (mostly) not even true. This also limits our ability to 'think outside the box'. Not only are we not able to think outside the box by doing this, we are actually boxing ourselves in. But there are ways to escape this 'negative problem trap'.

There is a brand of therapy called Solution-Focused Brief Therapy pioneered by Steve de Shaza and Inso Kim Berg. One technique is the use of something called The Miracle Question. Using our ability to creatively visualise the answer to this question allows us to focus on what would be different in our lives if the problems were not there. And it can help us see what our preferred future might look like. The power of this is that we don't even need to know or acknowledge what the problems are. Sounds strange? I thought so too before I became involved in Solution-Focused Brief Therapy. Up until then I believed it was absolutely necessary to comprehensively define the nature of the problem before even attempting to seek solutions. I discovered I was wrong. Have a go at the following; it might well work for you.

I recommend grabbing a piece of paper or recording your answers on your phone. Some people like to draw a picture of their answer – cartoons and stick people are fine. Sometimes the answers can be quite fresh and innovative. It would be a shame for them to slip away. A variation on the Miracle Question might be something along the lines of the following.

Imagine tonight, when you have gone to bed and are asleep, something happens. Call it a miracle if you like. This miracle gets rid of all the problems and restrictions that are getting in the way of you living your ideal life. You don't need to know or think about what the problems are or even what your ideal life might be. Of course, because you are asleep you don't know that this miracle has happened, nor does anyone else. So, when you wake up you have no idea that there has been a change. Ask yourself this question, "What is the first thing I would notice, however small, to show me that something was different?" It is really important to focus only on those things that you would actually notice.

This sounds so simple doesn't it. I have tried this literally hundreds of times with people of all ages; individuals and families. Some find it quite easy, some struggle. You might actually look at it and think, well that's just stupid; I know a miracle isn't going to happen, so what is the point? Well the point is that it takes our thinking process to a new and different place and helps us to think in a different way. It is almost like stepping into a time machine to a future we haven't thought of yet – a better future. A preferred future. This is possibly the future that we might get to if we only had control of the little origami paper boat floating down the stream. You might 'wake up' the morning after the miracle and notice that not much around you has changed a great deal. On the other hand, you might wake up in a very different place and a world that looks and feels very different. Write down, or draw, what it is that you notice that is different; you might be surprised and come up with things you might not have otherwise thought of.

Try an imaginary day in the life exercise

This is not quite the same as the Miracle Question. In the Miracle Question we were using our imagination to observe what we would notice that was different after waking up with problems gone (without even needing to define what the problems might be). With the Day in the Life we are going to decide on a number of possible preferred alternative futures and try them on for size. This is not daydreaming as such. Rather you are going through how a day might actually be and considering both positives and negatives, advantages and disadvantages. To stop yourself drifting too much you can draw up a log to fill in. Morning afternoon and evening along the left (or even by the hour). Then along the top three columns; what I am doing, whether it matches my values or not (how congruent is it?), and other comments. Think about what will be better about my life, and what will be worse about my life. Don't shy away from the negative aspects of your new future. Remember that we are looking to consider our alternatives against how congruent we will become. This means we must consider both circles of the congruency test.

Have a look at the diagram on the next page. I have drawn up a very basic log.

Time	Activity	Congruent?	Comment
Morning	Get up really early to feed horses	I hate early mornings (3/10)	It is worth it when I get to be with the horses
Afternoon	Ride out into the countryside	This is my number one value (10/10)	This alone makes it all worthwhile. Fantastic
Evening	Evening work in the distribution centre	Mindless work I don't really enjoy (4/10)	It may be mindless, but it is stress free and it pays the bills. I can bear it until I can become self-employed and do something else

Imagine our dream is to be to be with horses and be able to ride out free into the countryside each day. On our Miracle Question day we might see ourselves in a log cabin (or a massive ranch) with a stable next door. We simply hop onto our horse and ride off. We can check out the congruency value of this, and it comes out pretty high. However, when we start to look at a Day in the Life we can start to play with some of the variables. For example, I know that I need a job to pay the bills. I also know that I can't work during the day and ride a horse out into the countryside at the same time. So what if I took one of the evening shifts at the local warehouse? How would that feel, and would it be worth it? By writing it out you can examine some of the options. You can also look at the less congruent aspects and see if there might be any alternatives. For example, I have known people do a 'horse share' where they can split both the responsibilities and the pleasure and work this into a schedule. Or would this be even more incongruent than the first option? Only you can make such a judgement.

Go back and re-visit each of your childhood dreams.

I mentioned earlier that we find it more difficult to access our thoughts about our true values and beliefs as we get older. We start to shut off certain avenues as even being possibilities to explore, "What is the point in thinking about that, it's impossible". So put yourself back to a point where you were able to think and dream big and nothing seemed impossible. Maybe you wanted to be an astronaut, a train driver, a famous actor etc. When Elizabeth II, Queen of England, was once asked as a little girl what she wanted to be when she grew up. She famously replied, "A Horse". She was completely besotted with horses at that time, so that would be a perfectly acceptable answer for a child. Of course she continued her love of horses and this also rubbed off on her children. So don't even discount your most 'childish' fantasies. Being a horse might give you a congruency value of 10/10, but be impossible. However, being with horses might be 9/10 and patently not impossible.

Take yourself back to when you were a child and explore the answer you would have given about your preferred future back then. Also have a think about what your values were then. Dare I say it, before those values were jaundiced and twisted by the realities of 'the real world' and our experience of growing-up. The more values you write at this stage the better. You can either rank them out of 10 straight away or go back and rank them once they are written out. Categorise them based on the different elements of life list we looked at earlier when you did your first congruency test. Also, doing a Life Audit can be a good way of reactivating memories of childhood dreams and our previous ideas and hopes of the future. The first section of Part Two gives an example Life Audit to help with how this might look.

Try something completely different

In order to really stretch your imagination try some of the above exercises with something completely different, outlandish even. Maybe play around with some ideas that are things you know you wouldn't like, or are way out of your comfort zone. For me this would include things like becoming a surgeon (I am very squeamish), or a dancer (no coordination or ability to remember even the simplest sequence of steps). Sometimes getting a clear picture of what you don't like, and why, can help your internal discussion and thought processes. You can even think "what could I do to make my life worse". Getting your imagination to work for you and actually doing these exercises is vital. Our imagination is a very powerful 'muscle'. And like all muscles it can grow weak and start to atrophy if we don't exercise it.

By the way, you will probably start to have a few slightly weird dreams as you start to explore these new areas. Don't worry about it, and don't try and interpret them. Part of the dreaming process is when the brain starts to sort out and file away the experiences of the daytime and turns them into narrative memories that can be accessed again. Your night time filing system will have a lot to do once you start to explore these new 'preferred future' ideas. And the more your brain works in this way, and makes new connections, the easier you will find it to let your imagination loose in imagining your preferred congruent future.

Pulling it all together

What we are doing here is simply running through a number of possible future options and seeing which ones fit with who we are as a person. This is a vitally important step in figuring out what we want to do with our one life. We are starting with a wide range of possible options and then gradually narrowing them down based solely on whether they have a high congruency score for us. What we are not doing is simply dismissing things, or not even considering them simply because we think they might be difficult, unreachable, or be things we CANNOT do. As we start to go through this process we do not want to rule anything out at the early stages no matter how outlandish the different preferred future options may seem. We need to go through a process of sieving and sorting in order to find and choose our preferred future. This is similar to panning for gold. If you were panning for gold you wouldn't get far if you took a small pair of tweezers and started to pick away at the sand at the bottom of the stream hoping to see tiny little specs of the rare metal. Instead, you would start by looking in a likely area, then you would shovel up buckets of sand and rocks and mud and start to sort, and sift, and sieve, and shake, and examine what you had until eventually you were left with a few small nuggets of what you were looking for. The ideas and techniques described above combined with the notion of checking for congruency are what will help you move closer and closer to being able to see a future life that you want to actively choose and achieve. In doing this you are viewing the possible prospective future choices of what you might want to do and assessing them against how congruent they might be. This is the way that you can see whether any of these choices might actually work for you in reality.

This is what is known as an iterative process, which simply means that you will need to go through it a number of times as you get closer and closer to your desired goal of figuring out where you want to take your life. Take all of your congruency checking exercises, miracle days etc and see what patterns start to emerge. This is where your colourful notes and drawings will help. Draw up a congruency diagram based on the things you see emerging from your efforts. This should start to give you a good yardstick to measure any options that start to come to mind. You might find that your ideas on a preferred future are becoming very clear, specific and concrete, or you might find that they are quite abstract and general. You might also find that you come up with a few different options that each seem to fit your preferred future congruency test. You might have a list of possibilities that are closely related, or a list of quite disparate options. That is perfectly OK. At this stage it is the amount of congruency that is important.

We are not necessarily looking to come out with one clear specific defined choice or option. For example it might start to become clear to you that you really do want to become your own boss. That is actually more important than what it is you would actually be doing to earn a living. You might have come up with a few options to go along with that; having my own coffee shop, selling books, baking cakes etc. Now it may be possible to come up with something that combines all of these (I did once live in a village that had a combined coffee and book shop where they made their own cakes), or maybe any one of them would do. You may want to be your own boss, but also high up in your list is to live in a remote location. In this instance some sort of internet business (assuming you can get the internet) might work out. Or, you might want to work with animals, and there are several options that would be congruent for you; volunteer at a cat rescue centre, dog walking, raising alpaca, veterinary nursing, or being a racehorse trainer. List these out in order of congruence, they might all make a perfectly acceptable future for you. You might also find that you start to see a pathway of how to move from where you are now to where you want to be. For example, doing dog walking and volunteering at a cat rescue centre might help you as you move towards your key goal of becoming a veterinary nurse.

However it is possible that as you move through the sifting process, you unearth a very specific preferred future. This might be the re-kindling of a childhood dream that you uncovered during your Life Audit.

We will look at how to move from this list of options to the reality of actually choosing what to do when we go through the next section. And who says that you can only do one thing with your one life? You might decide that you wish to pursue a few different options – and these can either run at the same time or after one another.

If this is your first time reading through this book then keep on reading to the end of the next two sections. What you have read up to now will become even more relevant once you have read through the sections on actually making it all happen. If it is your second time then you will have tried the exercises covered above. In any case, at the end of each section I will finish with a few things for you to try. Do try them. They won't work if you don't. And if they are 'useful' then 'use' them, and keep using them.

Nine things to do

I would advise, again, having a notebook where you can jot ideas down. Our brain tends to remember ideas and things that are repeated. Unfortunately with new and novel ideas, they can slip out of our memory grasp quite quickly. That is really frustrating. Having a record of your thoughts as you go through the processes in this book will prove invaluable. And as I said before, drawing, cartoons and scribbles are fine. Stick-people with thought bubbles can be a very effective way of jotting down our thoughts.

1. Read through the rest of this book and then come back to this section if this is your first time through.
2. Think about which stage you are in from the States of Change model. Write a quick statement on where you are now, why you think that, and where you might go next.
3. Have a go at an initial Life Audit. This is best done after reading through the rest of this book, including the example life audit in Part Two.
4. Have a go at the "what would I do if I won the lottery?" question. Now this is one that you can do twice. First time right now on your first read through and then again after reading through the rest of this book and getting back to this section. Compare your two answers. You'll know why when you have been through the Aphorisms section.

5. Do a congruency test of where you are right now. Check back earlier on how to do this. Remember to use the lists and circles.
6. Do the same with a CANNOT list. Write down all those things you can think of that fit this category. Cross out those things that really are outside of your control. Consider what to do with what is left; should some of them go on the list of things you value. Have a look at what you have crossed out. Are you spending time worrying over these things? Remember that the secret of life is to only concern yourself with things you can do something about. Gently tell yourself to let these things go. You now have more time to think about what you want to do with your life.
7. Ask yourself the Miracle Question. Set aside some time to do this. Be in a place where you can get some peace and quiet for yourself. Walk around, talk to yourself out loud. Really put yourself into the morning after the miracle and really try and notice what is different. Be sure to write it down in some way. Do this a few times over the next week or so.
8. Try a visualisation of some random futures. Do a day in the life of things both inside and outside of your comfort zone.
9. Start to draw up a new congruence check based on your developing preferred future (or futures). Jump into a pretend time machine (or a real one if you have one) and look at your life as if you were already living in your preferred future. This is an iterative process. Let it settle and come back to it a few times. How comfortable does it feel? What would it be like if this was real? Is this what I want to do with my One Life? Let your 'future self' talk to your 'current self' and describe how much better the

new 'preferred future' is over the old drifting down the river 'present self'. Record this 'conversation' in some way, it will be useful later.

How do I get there?

In this section we will look at how we can actually make our preferred future happen. Now before we go any further, if this is the first time you are reading through this book, then you possibly don't have a particularly clear view of the specifics of where you want to take your life yet. Or maybe you do. Or maybe you have several alternatives, but don't know which one, or ones, to pursue. In any case, once you have read through this section you will almost certainly want to rewind a bit and use some of the things that come up to feed back into the first part of the process where you are exploring what your preferred future should look like. And this section will also help you in your decision as to which of your options to follow. But, wherever you are in the process, let's have a look at the bit that most people think is going to be the most difficult bit – how to actually make it happen in reality.

So, what might you be saying to yourself at this point? Possibly something along the lines of; I have imagined I only have one life, and have decided what I want to do with it. Unfortunately I don't have a clue how I can get from where I am now to where I want to be, and I am not even sure it is possible. Gosh this is difficult already and I haven't even started yet. I know what; I'll give up right now. Ouch, that's not a very positive way to start this section is it? Actually, it is simply being honest. That is how most of us feel when we have a massive task in front of us. We stare at the mountain we have to climb, we feel the initial enthusiasm and energy drain out of us, and then we pack up and go home. Yes, I will be using the notion of climbing a mountain as a metaphor quite a lot in this section. Sometimes the task ahead of us really can appear as difficult as climbing a mountain.

By the way, what you will discover in a few pages is that you have already started on the path of getting to where you want to be. By working through the first part of this book you have already completed a vital part of the journey and taken quite a few steps in the right direction – it just might not feel like that yet.

Where should we start? What do we need to do now, and what do we need to do next? Any task can feel massive if it is new and means that we have to make changes. Also, if we have gone through the previous section and are overjoyed with the realisation that what we really want to do is to realise our childhood dream and become; a nurse, a concert pianist, cycle round the world, be a foster carer, run a cat sanctuary, open our own coffee shop, make documentary films, become a full time artist, spend more time with the children, keep bees, or sit on a boat in a Scottish loch and write philosophy books (yes that really was one of mine – and maybe it still is). We will probably tell friends and family at this point expecting them to be overjoyed on our behalf. Unfortunately this does not always happen. There will be plenty of people who are willing to crush our dreams and tell us it is impossible, we are being stupid, we are too old, too young, it is a pipe dream etc. They might try and get us to put our plans on the CANNOT pile. You should be very wary of this.

Dealing with negativity from others is important. We don't live in isolation, and people are always willing to give their opinions. Sometimes supportive, often not. Remember that if you make a change in your life it could well mean that things will change in someone else's life as well. You might be excited about your idea of moving to a Yurt on the coast and living off the land in a minimalist way whilst making and selling sea-shell jewellery to tourists. Your friends or colleagues might genuinely think this is madness. They might also be considering that they will see less of you and may be losing a good friend. They might be jealous of your dream and believe that they could not do this themselves (remember that they have a CANNOT list as well). So what to say to them? Well firstly don't get into an argument. You don't have to justify yourself. A true friend will be supportive and could be a good ally as you move towards realising your dream. In the meantime, here is one of my favourite aphorisms that I use all the time and encourage others, as well as myself, to live by

"If you can't be the sun, don't be a cloud"

This can be a useful and simple reply to the negative people who will try and crush your dreams before they even get started. Say it with a smile. You might be amazed at the effect it can have.

How many people have you spoken to who can tell a tale of when they went to their careers advisor at school only to have all the enthusiasm knocked out of them? What I really wanted to do was be a {insert your dream here}, but my careers advisor said; that's not a job for, girls, boys, it's too risky, most people fail, it is totally unrealistic, "blah blah blah". I have heard numerous people tell me this story. It's not always the career advisor. Sometimes it is a teacher or parent. It has certainly happened to me and I am sure it has happened to many of you reading this. Unfortunately what then happens is that several years later we regret not having tried to go for our dream and then we convince ourselves that we are too old, it is too late. We put it into the CANNOT pile. And maybe it shouldn't really be in that pile at all, but hopefully you will have discovered this after working through the previous section.

But notwithstanding what others think. We still need to do some thinking, planning and then doing in order to make our lives what we want and stop drifting along like an origami boat in a stream.

The areas we will cover in this section are:

1. Turning a destination into a journey.

This starts by getting us into the right way of considering how we will approach this task of getting to where we want to be. And by 'this task' I mean the whole process of both planning and doing. Firstly, we need to get into a new way of thinking and consider each day of our path towards getting to where we want to be as being both the journey to our destination, and part of the destination itself. Then we need to turn our destination into a journey. I know that this sounds strange (in fact you probably read through that bit twice didn't you), and maybe a bit up in the clouds. But bear with me, I really will explain what this means and why it is vitally important.

2. Formulating your objectives

We will then look at how we can turn our aims and goals into workable objectives. We need a bit of a route map. Things we 'want' to achieve. And things we 'need' to achieve if we are going to live our lives the way we want to. And don't worry I am not going to get hung up on definitions of 'goal', 'aim', 'objective, and other pseudo management terms. I have been to several motivational seminars where the speaker has become very uptight in defining such terms (often in a way different to the previous seminar speaker) as if grasping these concepts alone are enough to make it happen – and they usually struggle to define what "it" is anyway. And if you have heard of so called 'SMART' goals (Specific, Measurable, Achievable, Realistic, Timescale), don't worry, these will only be discussed in the context of why they may or may not be useful for what you want to achieve. In brief, however you decide to formulate your objectives the vital thing is to check that they are aligned with your values to ensure that your future life will be a congruent one.

3. How to plan my journey

We will next look at how to plan our journey towards our preferred future. Yes, we do need a plan. This is not like a rigid project plan like the sort we would need if we were building a new chemical plant, or even more difficult, assembling some flat-pack furniture. But we do need to get a clear vision of what needs to happen; what we actually need to do, to get to where we want to be. It is also good to build in some flexibility. The unexpected can come up and try and divert us. We might even have to tolerate some gaps in our plan where we don't quite know what will happen until we get there. And the key question we need to be able to answer when we start to actually implement our plan is, "What do I need to do today?" This can sound very trivial. In fact it is of vital importance. It is actually quite easy to break our plan up into where we want to be in a 5 years, 2 years, 12 months, a fortnight, even next week etc. But to get anywhere, we need to know what is necessary to do right now. And the basic planning period for 'right now' is today – that period between the time we woke up this morning and the time we will go back to sleep again tonight.

4. Maintenance

We also need to review on a regular basis how things are going. Am I still on track? Is it working? Am I still being congruent? We might discover new things about ourselves on the journey that we couldn't have possibly known before we set out. This might have an impact on our preferred future and our overall goal. Maintenance simply means checking that we are still on track and going in the direction we want.

We will finally sum up with a selection of nine things to do before moving on to the final section of Part One of this book, mysteriously entitled Aphorisms and how to use them.

So let's get going and start off with a very important concept that might seem a bit strange at first. Namely, turning our destination into a journey.

Turning my destination into a journey

This is an important concept, but on the face of it, it does sound a little glib. "Life is not a destination, it's a journey" etc. I'm sure you've heard that one before. If you have ever watched a TV talent show people always talk about being 'on a journey'. Whereas we all know that they have really got their eye on the big prize, whatever that might be; money, a recording contract, fame? So what do I mean when I talk about turning a destination into a journey, and why would we want to do that anyway? Let us have a look at a few examples. If my aim is to spend a weekend in Venice, Italy, that's what I want to do, and Venice is where I want to be. It is my destination. If someone had invented a teleporter machine I would probably use that to get there (By the way, if you are reading this in 2130 and there are personal teleporters on every street corner, then you probably won't understand this analogy). Failing that, we would probably look for the quickest or cheapest flights. If we can't afford that, then we might look at trains, busses, coaches or even hitch-hiking. There is no problem with any of this, and I am sure you will have a great time visiting St Mark's Square and floating along on a gondola eating ice cream. But, imagine you had wanted to do this 200 years ago. Think of how different that would have looked. The journey itself (depending on where you were starting from) would have been a massive part of the whole venture. In fact surviving the journey would have probably been a big goal in its own right.

We often use 'mountain' metaphors in our normal speech when talking about life changes, so let's have a look at a few now. What if your long term dream was to conquer Mount Everest? Think about how fulfilling, or not, it would be to get dropped off out of a luxuriously appointed helicopter for a 20 minute stop at the summit (I do know that technically this is not possible for all sorts of reasons). Is this really "conquering" Everest? I would suggest that this was probably not very fulfilling, and you might not feel that your dream had actually been realised. Mind you, if your dream was simply to stand on the top of Mount Everest and admire the view, then maybe the helicopter could be an option. I am going to keep on with a climbing analogy for a couple of paragraphs. We do sometimes thing of approaching a new venture as akin to climbing a metaphorical mountain.

Joe Brown and George Brand were the first people to conquer Mount Kanchenjunga on May 25th 1955. Mount Kanchenjunga is very remote and lies on the border between Nepal and Sikkim, India. Until trigonometry technology was perfected around 1850 it was assumed to be the highest mountain in the world. Once the height was measured more accurately it then slipped back to third place behind Everest and K2. So not Everest, but still a pretty big mountain nevertheless. Brown and Brand would have spent months planning their expedition and then probably weeks climbing. They did well and got to within a couple of feet of the actual summit, and stopped. They did not set foot on the fresh surface on the actual peak of the mountain. There was no physical barrier stopping them. So why didn't they take the few extra steps? Well, have a think about why you consider this might be and then only afterwards do an internet search – or pop down to your local library. Thinking about the different reasons why they didn't is a useful mental exercise and possibly even more useful that simply knowing the answer. I will 'hide' the answer elsewhere in this book, but in the meantime think about life-values, and not just those of Brown and Brand. Importantly, they are still considered to be the first people to "conquer" Mount Kanchenjunga even though they didn't actually stand on the top of it.

But it was worth it for them. They had achieved their goal, and a major part of achieving that was the planning element which made reaching the destination possible. Their journey and destination were actually part and parcel of the same thing in practice. And remember, that they also needed to get down again. It is very unlikely that Brown turned to Brand when they were at the 'top' and said, "Excellent, we made it, that was so worth all the planning and effort – oh hang on, how do we get back down? We didn't think of that". So, the journey is not just the 'bit' before the destination, it can also be the 'bit, after the destination.

However, the important thing here is that we should not decide what our preferred future would look like and then simply decide what the problems are we need to get rid of to get there; and then blindly work to get rid of those problems. This can lead to us having a horrible time right now as we punish ourselves to get to the end goal, telling ourselves, "It will be worth it in the end". For a lot of parents their chosen destination might be to selflessly do whatever they can to give their children a good start in life. This is what they have chosen to do with their one life; to give their children the best life possible. Well, there is nothing wrong with that is there! But, how many people do you know who work every hour they can to earn money to buy their family things and make their children's futures' a better place. Sometimes even chastising their children as if it was their fault, "Do you know the sacrifices I've made for you?" Then one day they turn around, the children are adults and have left home. They never really got to know them and the adult children don't really have any reason to now get to know their parent. Yes, I know, this is the exact story of "The cat's in the Cradle" written and sung by Harry Chapin in 1974. If you don't know it, look it up. It contains painful truths for many people.

Here is another tiny bit of Philosophy, and one of the first Aphorisms that I picked up and found useful. – Something along the lines of, 'Humans are an ends in themselves and never a means to an end'. This is from Immanuel Kant who was a German writing around the mid 1700's. In addition to some very complex philosophy regarding reason, logic and free-will, he also wrote about ethics and morality. One of his conclusions is that when dealing with others we should treat people as an ends in themselves and never as a means to an end. This is sort of saying that we shouldn't trample over others in order to get we want. Other people should not be simply regarded as potential collateral damage in my quest to reach my goal. Other people have their own dignity and worth and that dignity and worth must be taken into account as I move through life in the pursuit of getting to where I want to be. You might be nodding at this and thinking that it sounds reasonable. If you broadly agree with this, then let's take it one stage further. You (yes you, the individual person reading this book) are as much a human as those around you. So you shouldn't use yourself as a means to an ends either. You shouldn't trample on yourself in order to get what you want. You have worth, dignity and values and these should not be discarded as you move on your journey to your destination. In fact, there should be no discrepancy or difference in the way you apply your values between the journey and the destination. We have already figured out that we want a congruent preferred future. But our path to that future is also part of our future, so we need to start to see the path as being subject to the same values that are guiding us to where we want to be. Was that a bit too philosophical? I apologise if it was. So let's get back down to earth a bit.

But hang on, you might be saying, surely we need to make some difficult sacrifices now in order to get where we want to be in the future. Yes, we might well need to go through a period that is difficult. In fact, going through almost any change is difficult. The first 30 days of any change, even a good one, can be difficult. In reality there is no way that we can simply start being totally congruent from day one. However, a very important part of our planning process is to set objectives that can be measured against congruence. And by 'measured', I mean on a simple scale of 0 to 10 (0 being totally incongruent and 10 being totally aligned and congruent). So, for example I might need to continue an incongruent office or warehouse job for a while (simply to pay the bills) as I move other parts of my life towards congruency (doing an evening class in furniture restoration for example). The key being that by monitoring the congruency of what we are doing as we move towards our preferred future, we are not just drifting with the current; we are actually in charge of steering our little origami boat along the stream. It is true that we may prefer to be floating in a placid stream of crystal clear water with fragrant flowers covering the banks, but if we are up against the rocks being battered by the current, then we need to do what it takes to steer from the rocks, and that might mean being somewhat incongruent for a while. However, if we only focus on where we want to get to we can start to lose all perspective on everything else that is important. There is only so long that you can live a non-congruent life before the two circles of Who I Am and What I Do start to become so far apart that Who I Am no longer gets a look in, and we lose sight of why we set of on this route in the first place. And one of the reasons for making changes to get to where we want to be, is because out current lifestyle is not congruent.

When we plan how to get to the point where we are living the type of life we want, we have to bear in mind that we are still living a life, our one life, as we move towards that point. And this 'one life' as we move towards our 'end point' should be congruent and aligned with the values of the preferred future we are aiming for. Or at least as congruent as possible. We also need to consider what we are going to do when we get to our goal. In the case of Joe Brown and George Brand they simply wanted to get back down the mountain safely as they had other mountains on their conquering to-do list. However, we don't want to simply get to where we want to be then go into reverse and end up back where we started. I don't think I have met any dieters who have said, "Yes, I wanted to lose a lot of weight, it took me 6 months to reach my target and now I have put it all back on and I am back at the weight I started at. I have been so successful; now I am going to give up smoking for a few months before going back to 3 packs a day". This really doesn't make sense does it? It is so easy to focus only on the goal and lose perspective on everything that comes before and after it.

When you looked at what you wanted to do with your (one) life in the first section you did consider what you would be doing and how it would be different. It is so important to do this. The big danger is to then forget that actually we do only have one life, and that one life is being lived right here and right now. Life is actually a process; it is a journey that we take one step at a time as we actually fill it with activities and experiences as we go through the process of living life from day to day.

OK, so here is the punchline. There is actually a huge benefit to this. Once we start to see our journey and destination as being the same thing (pretty much made of the same stuff – that 'stuff' being our life), we realise that we can actually not only change the path of our little origami boat down the river – we can actually start to change the path of the river itself. As noted before, the secret of life is to only concern ourselves with those things that we can change and not spend fruitless time and energy devoted to worrying and regretting those things that we can't change. However, you may find that you can have more influence over the possible direction of your life than you ever thought. Maybe your CANNOT list is not as long as you previously thought. Very often this is simply a matter of confidence. I have seen many people I have worked with start to gain confidence as they learn to manage their anxieties and start to do things they would have otherwise avoided. They start to do things that they would have previously thought impossible ("for people like me"). Think back to our example of wanting to conquer Everest. What do you think you would have gained more from, standing on the top, or the experience of planning the journey and doing the climb? I would wager that you would see it all as one amazing life-changing experience. Our destination and every part of our journey are effectively the same thing. It is the same regarding our 'one life'. We can figure out that we want to get to somewhere different from where we are today, but on our way there we are still living that same 'one life'.

Formulating my life objectives

I am not going to get too hung up on terms like 'goal' and 'objective' etc. Some might argue that in setting a plan we have an overall objective and we set smaller interim goals we need to accomplish in order to get there. Some might argue conversely that we have one specific goal and we need to successfully complete a number of interim objectives in order to get there. Each one of these goals or objectives is seen a destination (or a stop-off point) in its own right. Such concepts might be great for some business planning projects or building a new factory, but this way of looking at things does not necessarily translate well into the way we should formulate or describe what we want to do with our one life.

Think back on some of those examples in the previous sections where we wished for something to be different, but didn't really consider what we would be doing (with our lives) that was different. Let us take a very common example that many people have as a 'goal'. I apologise if this example does not apply to you, but if it doesn't then you almost certainly know someone who it does fit. And I am sure you will be able to follow it. The example is that I might want to lose weight. Many people, including myself, have had this wish at some point in their lives.

There is a whole industry out there telling us how to do this. There are diets, mutual support groups, products (for example the 'Abs' machines mentioned earlier), and hundreds of books and videos. Now, I have not tried all the approaches, but apart from the really bizarre regimes (anyone remember the donut diet? – I do; it didn't work for me and that wasn't the result of me not trying), most of them probably work if you stick to them. And for some of the more enlightened weight loss regimes, there is now more focus on helping you to be able to stick to them than there was previously.

But a lot of people do 'fail'. So why might that be? We should take a slight diversion at this point and talk a bit about so called "secondary gain". This is where we hide from ourselves the fact that failing to overcome the 'visible' problem we think we want to solve is actually helping us to avoid an 'invisible' problem that is our real problem or fear, and which we are avoiding even thinking about. If we fail to solve the visible problem then we never have to confront the invisible one. So failing in this sense is actually helping us to succeed in a strange way as it means we will never have to face the real problem. So, 'secondary gain' is the benefit we get from continuing to not overcome the problem we are trying to solve. The 'invisible problem' is the real one that is so dark and scary that we don't even want to acknowledge it. We hide it with the 'visible problem'.

For example, I might think that me being overweight and unfit is what is holding me back from promotion at work. The successful people at work all seem to go out jogging together and meet at the tennis club. Therefore all I need to do is start jogging and cut down on calories. Within a few months I will have my promotion and be part of the tennis clique. Unfortunately, try as I might, I don't seem to be able to resist the carbohydrate loaded high

84

calorie meals, and besides, they have a 'special' 2 for the price of 1 on ice cream at the supermarket. And meanwhile my gym card is gathering dust on the sideboard (although I have swatted a few flies with my super expensive carbon fibre tennis racquet), there just never seems to be time to fit in a gym or tennis session, let alone three times every week. So, I focus and fail on trying to diet and get fit. That is the visible problem as I see it; me being unfit and overweight. However, there might be an invisible hidden problem that is actually the real one.

Failing to fix the visible problem is actually giving me 'secondary gain' because it means I don't have to face up to the bigger, real problem. So, what might the real problem be in this instance? It could be one of many things. Let's make up an example for the sake of illustration. Maybe I find the people at the tennis club boring and superficial, full of vacuous and shallow chit chat. Or maybe I think they are intellectually above me and I would be mocked for my lack of knowledge on current affairs. Maybe I hate tennis and would rather spend my spare time fishing or making quilts. Maybe I am actually scared that if I go for promotion I wouldn't be up to doing the new job. Maybe it is more comfortable for me to believe that I am not able to lose weight than it is for me to face a much bigger fear of a bigger job. Or maybe I don't really want the new more highly powered job. It would mean more pressure, less time with the family and lots of stress. It might take me further away from the things I really value and which make me congruent. Possibly I have been brought up to believe that I should always be striving to be successful by gaining promotion and earning more. Maybe I have never questioned this, and maybe just blindly following this path is taking me further and further away from me being congruent with who I am.

This is a good illustration of why it is important to really figure out what you really do want before setting off to try and get it. If you set your objectives in terms of getting rid of 'visible' problems without considering that they might be hiding 'invisible' ones you might just be falling into a trap.

However once you formulate your objectives in a more congruent way you can check and guard against hiding the real, but invisible, issues. Once you have done this, you might well decide that losing weight and becoming fitter is of value to you. But this time your desire to do this might come from a different place. One of your congruence values might be to spend more quality time with your children. When you look into your preferred future you might see yourself actively playing sports and running around with them. This is a different situation as there is no secondary gain from failing to lose weight and getting fit. This can have a massive impact on your motivation to help you actually achieve your goal. We will look at setting congruent goals in more detail when we use the technique of 'a letter from the future' in a few pages.

If you really were looking to lose weight and that is very important for you for reasons that fit in with your values and in line with your congruity, it is vital to choose a method or regime that fits you and your circumstances. It is also important to do it at a pace that suits your health and your lifestyle. There are risks to losing too much weight too quickly. It is possible to lose muscle – which weighs more than fat, but muscle is actually the engine that burns fat. We then get discouraged because the weight loss slows down. We go back to what we used to do.

Unfortunately we then put on weight quicker (not so much muscle to burn the fat) and become despondent. However, we pull ourselves together and go on another diet – maybe the same one, maybe a different one. And…you can see what happens next. This cycle repeats itself. You have probably heard the term, 'yo-yo dieting'. Well, this is what it is. I only added this paragraph because I did spend some time as a gym fitness instructor. I would always ask people what they wanted out of their fitness program. Many simply said that they wanted to "lose weight". A very typical reason for being at the gym is the first place is because I, "I am fat, forty, and fed up" (insert an alliteration of choice to fit your individual age and circumstance. But just getting the weight loss might not lead to feeling, "fit, forty and fabulous" on its own. Wanting to be "fit, forty and fabulous" is not the same thing as wanting to lose weight.

A different way of looking at it is to think about what we would be doing different once we had lost the weight. Very much along the lines of the Miracle Question in the previous section. What difference would it really make in practical terms? What would we notice that was different about the world? What would others notice that was different about us? (And I am not just talking about our waist measurement or dress size here). What would we notice that was different about what we were doing? Yes this is exactly what we looked at when we were considering what we wanted our 'preferred future' to look like in the last section.

So how should we formulate our life objectives? Well firstly, you have probably already guessed that any formulation of 'life objectives' should be in terms of both the journey and the destination. Have you ever started a car journey and considered if you should take the 'fast' route or the 'scenic' route'? I am quite lucky in that I live near the sea, and I am one of those people who derives a great deal of pleasure simply by watching the sea do what the sea does. Simply put, part of what makes my life congruent is being able to look at the sea. Some of life's most simple pleasures can also be the most important, and you may have discovered this when you did your congruency check in the last section. However, back to my choice of which route to take. When I drive to most destinations there is no need for me to actually drive along any of the coastal roads which would give me a good view of the sea. It is quicker not to go near the sea for almost all of the standard journeys I take. But I almost always choose to take the scenic route so that I can see what the sea is doing today. It makes my journey so much more pleasant and gives me a sense of well-being. I am not saying that we should always take the 'scenic' route in life, but we should definitely consider it and include it as part of the formulation of our goals.

You might well have heard of SMART goals. These are touted in all sorts of business planning processes and the concept is very good at focusing the mind. SMART goals are very destination focused. They don't really consider that the journey is also the destination in the way we have looked at earlier. I have seen SMART goals defined in different ways, but a common definition is that SMART goals should be:

S –   Specific. Be precise about what it is you want to achieve.

M -   Measurable. Define your goal in a way that it can be quantified.

88

A – Achievable. Not 'pie in the sky', but something that could actually be realised.

R – Relevant. In tune with other things (the business) we are doing or want

T – Timescale. The time frame in which to achieve the goal should be defined.

However, I have been to many business training meetings where the new trainer defines these terms differently from the previous trainer and then gets quite hot under the collar about using his or her precise definition of the SMART acronym and the terms it contains. Let's be honest about this. One of the appealing factors of going for SMART goals is that it is an appealing acronym; it sounds great, it sounds clever and well, "smart". Who doesn't want their goals to be 'smart' (clever, knowing, shrewd, adroit, ingenious, etc)? Of course, in an organisation or business it makes sense to ensure that everyone is working to the same set of definitions as we set our goals. I have seen a few projects going very pear shaped as different people and departments defined the SMART goals in different ways. See how many combinations of the following possible alternatives you can make – plus the original ones above of course:

S – Sensible, Significant, Stretching
M – Motivating, Meaningful
A – Agreed, Action-based, Attainable, Ambitious
R – Realistic, Rewarding, Results-Oriented
T – Tangible, Trackable, Time-Based, Testable

I don't want to dismiss SMART goals and, as long as everyone agrees with the definition of each letter in the acronym, they can provide a very good framework for clarifying and tracking projects, even climbing a mountain possibly. And all of the different terms above can be useful ones to toy around with as we develop how to get to our preferred future. However, we also need something that is going to allow us to integrate the journey and destination as being the same thing.

Right, so the really good news is that you have already done 90% of the work involved in formulating your objectives. This is pretty much what we were doing in the 'what do I want to do?' section. The formulation of our life objectives is also part of the answer to, "Imagine you only had one life. What would you do with it?" So, if this is your second time of reading through this book and you have already done the exercises in the first part you will have already completed the first and most important goal formulation. You will have 'painted' a picture of a new preferred future and checked that it is congruent and in line with your values. Hopefully you will have written this down or recorded it in some way. By doing this the way that we did (or more correctly, the way that you did) we have already ensured that our goals meet the majority of the different SMART goal definitions above. I'll jumble them up a bit, but you will certainly have considered at least the following, rewarding, achievable, sensible, tangible, meaningful, significant and motivating. In fact, the only bit that is possibly missing is the timeframe.

Timeframe is a complex issue when it comes to life planning. There are two really key planning periods. The first and obvious one is 'a lifetime' (my one lifetime). The second and much less obvious one is 'today' (that period between waking up this morning and going to sleep tonight). My lifetime is totally personal to me and is the thing that I only have one of. It stretches out behind me in terms of the things I have already done and experienced; that part is to a great extent already known to me. My lifetime also stretches out in front of me; it is the bit I want to shape into my new and preferred future. But, "today" is where I actually live. It is only the things that I do today that will have an effect on shaping my future, and it is only by doing those things today that I choose to do that I can shape my future the way I want.

Now, at this point you might argue that I am actually the sum total of everything that has happened to me up to this point and that my past experiences have made me the person I am today. I would not dispute that, but I would say that you can make a choice as to whether you become a prisoner of your past, or whether you simply acknowledge your past and then decide what you want to change as you move into the future. In part, this is why it can be useful to do a Life Audit as noted earlier. In truth, simply because I made decisions (or didn't make decisions and just drifted along) the way I did before doesn't mean I have to make the same decisions time and time again – or even make decisions in the same way.

Remember the two fundamental questions of life we covered earlier in the book. "What is the secret of life?" and "What is the meaning of life?" We discussed that the 'secret' is to only concern yourself with things you can do something about. Well, you can't change what happened in your past. But maybe in your past you did concern yourself a lot with things you couldn't actually change. Now that you realise this, you can move on and do things differently having learnt a valuable lesson.

Likewise the 'meaning' of life is to actively seek out a life that is my authentic life. In short to move towards a life that is congruent where my values and what I do are aligned. Maybe in the past you were being very incongruent. Again, you can't change what happened in the past. But now realising this you can start to do things differently having learnt a valuable lesson. Or maybe you discover times in your past when you were very congruent. Possibly you didn't even notice this at the time; you simply regarded them as happy times. You can learn valuable lessons from these times and they can help you examine what might need to happen for you to bring congruence back into your life.

This is where doing a Life Audit can be useful. But use it as a learning exercise to move forward. Don't spend time beating yourself up over past mistakes. And because what happened in your past is not something you can do anything about, spending time concerning yourself about it in a negative way would be ignoring the secret of life, and would not be useful at all. And remember we want what we do here to be useful.

And on the subject of being useful. It is very useful when formulating your goals to record them in some way. The aim is to describe your objectives in the same way that you would describe any important and pleasant thing that happens in your life. The description should be alive, vibrant and recognisably different from what is going on for you today. You will have already done this as you went through the '9 Things to Try' at the end of the last section. How you do this is up to you, but I would recommend doing a combination of the following:

- Write them down. A bullet point list or a narrative description.

- Draw a picture. Realistic, or abstract, possibly a river with new preferred stopover points and nice scenery.
- Record your voice on your phone, describe each goal in terms of what you will be doing.
- Video yourself. Literally just sit in front of the camera and describe your new future.

So let us have a look at some guidelines of what to include as we formulate our objectives.

One really good way of doing this is a quite often used motivational approach of a 'letter' from the future. This can also be a video, voice recording, or drawing from the future. Basically you write a letter to yourself and from yourself as if you were already at a point in time where you are actually living your preferred future – you have already met your goals, and are living a congruent life. This letter can also be developed further to help to keep your motivation, avoid procrastination, and guide you as to what you need to do "today". We will cover this later. As an example, my letter from the future based on my previously stated notion that I might want to be sitting on a boat in a Scottish Loch writing philosophy books might look a bit like this:

"To me

Dear me

I am sitting here on my boat writing this to you on a lovely sunny day. I am anchored in the most peaceful and quiet loch in Scotland with only the occasional sound of the birds calling out as they fly around me and the gentle sound of the water lapping against the hull of the boat. I have just poured myself a cup of freshly brewed tea as a reward for finishing my third book in the short series of central philosophical ideas. I am very pleased with this one and can't wait to get it published. This one was on the notion of free will and self-determination and I am about to choose the title and get a cover designed. There is something about the smell of the Scottish heather wafting across the water that really frees up my mind and the ideas just seem to flow. I think I might take the dinghy to shore later and have a long walk. Tomorrow I will up-anchor and sail round to one of the other lochs as the weather is looking good for a really spirited sail to blow a few cobwebs away. I will then spend a leisurely time over the next few weeks researching for my next book which will be on the subject of personal rights and collective responsibility. Ah well, I must sign off now as the tea seems to be just about the right temperature to drink and I am going to take it up on deck and relax.

I am so glad that I chose to do this with my life and I wanted to write and thank you for sticking with it and making this all possible. At this very moment my congruency is at a 10/10. I am exactly where I want to be and doing exactly what I want to be doing.

Very Best Wishes

From me"

Did that seem a bit strange? Strange, both in terms of the actual dream and as a way of 'defining' a goal. Now for some of you it might not only have seemed strange, but totally scary. I know many people who hate being on boats, and many more who would find being alone on one in the middle of a deserted loch about as boring as it was possible to get. But this is my letter from the future. Yours would be completely different. The important thing is that it is alive, vibrant, describes things that are of value to me, and is demonstrably and recognisably different from what is happening right now. Try and really describe what you are

94

doing using as many of your senses as you can (what you see, hear, smell etc). Also put in some context – what you have just done, what you about to do etc. But write it mainly in the present tense as you would describe what you are doing at that very moment. Don't make it too long, but put in enough detail so that you are really describing a future congruent you. We will revisit this letter a bit later and see how it can be enhanced and used as a motivational tool to help plan the steps we need to get us to where we want to get to.

Here are a few guidelines of things that might be useful when you start to consider your objectives, and they can all then be used with a bit of modification in your letter from the future.

Describe each objective as the start of a new process rather than simply the end of a stage.

"When I reach objective 1 I will be doing......." Describe what you are actually doing.

Rather than "When I have reached objective 1, I will have finished X, Y, Z....." So not, "I will have learned to speak French", but rather, "I will be going to the weekly local French cultural exchange society meetings and conversing with other members in French".

Your description should be of something that is observable and recognisable by yourself and others. Using the above example, if you just looked at me sitting here, you would have no idea if I could speak French or not. But if you followed me into a French Patisserie in a small rural village in Brittany and witnessed me trying to buy some breakfast treats for the family, you would soon know whether I could speak French or not.

Your description of your objectives should also be linked to your congruency which is linked directly to how valuable this goal is to you. It is very useful to be able to describe objectives in such a way that you can put a number against them. Something that is scalable from 0 to 10. "0" meaning that this has not yet reached congruency at all, it is currently a million miles from where I want to be, and "10" means that you are there and what you are doing is completely lined up with your goal. So for example, imagine that one of your key values was to spend quality time with your family and children. And possibly at the moment you are working every hour possible and you only get to tuck the children up and kiss them goodnight after they have gone to bed. A laudable goal might simply be, "To spend more time with my children and family". But this doesn't really say what you will be doing differently once you have reached the goal; it is more or less simply repeating the words of your congruency key value. If we looked at this from the perspective of asking ourselves the Miracle Question, we might wake up after the miracle night and find that we were taking the children out somewhere fun for the day. So a goal that reflects what is valuable to us and also describes what we would be doing (that was different), might be along the lines of the following. "I will take my children somewhere fun every weekend". As you move towards this you might not manage every weekend, but you can start to measure (from 0 to 10) how close you are getting.

So linking the description of your goals back to the Miracle Question and congruency values is very important. You might have found the Miracle Question difficult when you first tried it. You might have even found it so quirky, weird and strange sounding that you didn't try it at all. I would encourage you to have a go and really imagine what it would be like to wake up on the morning after a 'miracle' had happened. Describe, write, video, or draw what you notice that is different, including what you are doing that is different. And also things that others might notice are different about you. This might not be as detailed as the letter from the future above, but it is a good start to allowing your imagination to explore options. Hopefully you can now see how the Miracle Question can be a good tool in helping to free up any constraints and start to see what a congruent preferred future could look like. I have used it many times in my professional life and seen how powerful it can be in helping people move on from where they are now to where they would prefer to be.

Oh, and by the way, sometimes you can start doing things from your preferred future straight away. Have a think about this and see if there are any changes you can make now. It doesn't matter how small the changes are, it is making the change that is important. Maybe you really can't take the children out every weekend at the moment as you are working seven days a week, but you could possibly book some special quality time with them each week and stick to it.

We should have a note about timeframes. You might have already started to think about this already. There is no harm in thinking about, "Where do I want to be, and what do I want to be doing this time next year?" Or, in five years' time, or even ten years' time etc. In part the questions around timeframe will be set by what it is we want to do, and where we want to get to. If I am making a career change that requires some specific re-training or gaining of some qualifications or experience then a small amount of research can help me understand this. I don't know off the top of my head what the timeframes for becoming a veterinary nurse, a dental hygienist, or an astronaut are for example. But I imagine that we might be talking many months or even years of training and study. And there might be months or years of study or experience that is needed before I even start the main study. I can imagine that to get on a veterinary nursing course you would need to demonstrate some previous experience of working with animals. There might even be a minimum requirement. This is certainly the case in the UK if you want to become a Clinical Psychologist; you need a degree in Psychology followed by some significant experience in clinical or research related work, and only then can you even apply for a Clinical Psychology course. I would imagine that becoming an astronaut has an even longer timeframe with a much more stringent set of pre-requisites. But just because the timeframe might be long, it doesn't mean that you shouldn't still follow your dream. And it doesn't matter what age you happen to be. Sure there might be some statutory restrictions. If you are 16 and you want to drive massive heavy goods trucks across Alaska you will probably not be allowed to do this until you are 21 (at least that is the UK age). And there may be an upper limit for some things – I am actually struggling to think of examples of upper ages as I have known people do the most extraordinary things well into their 80's and 90's (I was once overtaken by a 92 year old during the 2002 London Marathon! My excuse was that my knee had given out).

So, lets' get back to our veterinary nurse and use this as an example. This is one of the options that came from my preferred future list earlier. Maybe one of the things that makes my life congruent is being with animals and caring for them. Unfortunately, maybe I am currently living in a noisy city and taking the crowded subway train to a pressurised job selling insurance products to the construction industry over the phone. When I worked through the Miracle Question, I woke up on the morning after the overnight miracle and walked to my work at the veterinary practice across a field of cows next to a babbling brook. My first task was to check on and feed the animals who have stayed in overnight. I then checked the rota for today and saw that we had 3 minor operations lined up that I will be assisting...and so the day went on.

There is quite a gap between what I am doing 'now' and what I am going to be doing 'then'. We can see that the timeframe on this one might be quite long. There are also probably quite a lot of individual steps to take in our journey as we move from here to there. We might feel quite overwhelmed with the size of the mountain in front of us. Also, are we actually being realistic. Maybe becoming a veterinary nurse is realistic, but what if I wanted to become a world leading veterinary surgeon? There is a saying that we should aim for the stars and we will reach the moon. Being a world famous veterinary surgeon may give me a congruency rating of 10/10. But being a veterinary nurse might give me 9/10 and working part time as a volunteer at an animal shelter might be 8/10. But all are much more congruent than selling insurance over the phone that is only giving me a congruency rating of 2/10 at the moment. When I have asked a lot of people what number they would want to achieve I am quite pleasantly surprised that most say they would be very happy indeed to get to about 8/10. They say that this would bring them very real happiness and fulfilment. Have a think about what congruence level out of 10 you would need to achieve for your life to be truly happy and fulfilling.

Planning my journey

I am going to change the analogy a bit here. For the moment we are not on an origami boat, nor are we climbing a mountain. Planning our journey can also be like planning a passage on an old sailing boat. In days of yore they never used to say that they were sailing "to" somewhere. They would tend to say that they were sailing "towards" a particular destination. This is because they could never quite foresee all the possible weather combinations and forecasts. Weather predictions were more based on data and knowledge of typical averages from the last 10 years or so rather than the up to date satellite forecasts we can get on our smartphones today. In a similar way, we can't foresee or control everything in our life as we start our journey towards our goals.

Firstly we need to get a broad view perspective of where we are, where we are going and what might lie between 'here' and 'there'. What we need to do at this stage is draw up a general view of the main parts of the journey to the point where we have reached our preferred future. But with not too much detail at this stage. In fact delving into detail too early can cause us to panic a bit as we get embroiled in all the tiny details. Then we should start to identify key milestones. Milestones are those things that need to happen to progress us along our journey. Let us stick with our example of changing career aligned to a key value of wanting to work with animals. One possibility would be to become a Veterinary Nurse as noted above, but I am not sure how to do this.

Some basic internet searching will soon show us that (in the UK), this is a profession with protected status which means that I will need to qualify and become formally registered. Interestingly, there is more than one route to becoming a Veterinary Nurse; a University based one or a more practical one. So we immediately have a choice as to which journey towards our destination might be more congruent for us. Becoming qualified is therefore a major milestone which needs to be reached, but already we have at least two different paths to get there. Both with different timeframes.

There are a number of pre-requisites before I even start on whichever path. I must have a minimum number of qualifications in English, Math(s) and a Science subject. Getting these qualifications would be a milestone I would need to factor into my plan. However, there are also alternatives to this specific milestone. It is possible to start on the process to qualifying if I have an 'animal nursing assistant' (ANA) or 'veterinary care assistant' (VCA) qualification along with some other functional qualifications. So, I have even more options that I can start to map out and include as possible alternative milestones. If I am starting from zero I could go to night school and get the more formal qualifications if I don't have them already, or I could start working with animals immediately and get my ANA or VCA. Individual universities might have their own enrolment criteria if I decide to go down this route. So each milestone could have a mini-plan with options in its own right. As I noted earlier, it is important not to get too bogged down in detail at this point. Aim to get a general overall picture that you can visualise before getting into detail. Also, give yourself some time to research and understand what options are available to you. When I have researched similar things I have very rarely understood the 'official' route map of how to get to where I want to be. I usually have to draw it out (quite literally on a large sheet of paper) with all the options snaking off in different directions. And if there are different options like the ones above, then you can also spend some time considering which option might be more congruent for you. Some people might thrive on going down the intensive academic route. Others might want to get hands-on as soon as possible. A congruent plan for one person might not be congruent for another even if they both 'end' at the same destination.

Additionally, in this field we are using as an example there is a lot of competition to get either a vocational training place or a university place. I would need to prove that I have a real interest and significant experience of working with animals in order to get awarded a place. So, maybe this is something I need to incorporate into my plan right at the start and ensure that I can build up a good deal of evidence of practical involvement with animals. Getting this experience early on is therefore a key milestone, but is also something that is both part of the journey and a destination in its own right.

The above is not meant to be a definitive guide to becoming a Veterinary Nurse. But the type of pathways and options available are typical for a lot of skilled or professional career qualifications. It can be quite complicated, so it is worth doing some homework at this stage. But don't get too tied up or too despondent. Simply make a note of any of the key milestones and requirements you will need to be aware of. By the way, if you are reading this in the USA, there are many more different routes into veterinary nursing or becoming a veterinary technician – these are defined on a State by State basis although there are also national qualifications.

We can also identify any major hurdles and challenges that will need to be overcome at this stage. In the olden days our sea journey from one side of America to the other might have necessitated making the hazardous journey around Cape Horn. Nowadays we can take a short cut and go through the Panama Canal. Similarly in planning how to get to our preferred future, we might find that there actually are some shortcuts and help might be at hand to help us. Draw up a list and identify what resources you might be able to call on. You might be surprised at some of the skills you identified that you already have when you did your Life Audit. You might be making changes as a family in which case everyone will have their own specific skills they can bring to the process. Friends, neighbours and relatives could help too. In any case, get an idea of the 'crew' who will be helping you on your voyage.

Start to think about alternative destinations or stop-off points. Consider some 'what if' questions. Safe ports of call in case things do not go according to plan. What if I can't get to where I want to go in one single journey? If my key goal is to work with animals and I have turned my destination into a journey then as I work towards my long term goal (of becoming a veterinary nurse) maybe I can decide to take a planned stop-off. Maybe I can work as a volunteer at an animal sanctuary which is still congruent, but at the moment the timing is not quite right and I need to continue working to save for the time when I will be going back to full time study. Or maybe an opportunity might come up to start my own animal related business – this might fulfil two values of 'being my own boss' and 'working with animals'. This can lead to some quite tricky decisions as to whether I stick to the current plan or modify it. The key to approaching these decisions is to maintain fidelity with flexibility. This means to keep the fidelity of moving towards your congruent preferred future, but being flexible enough to consider other options and alternatives as they naturally arise.

Think about the things that might get in my way or stop me. Is Anxiety one of them? Having some degree of anxiety when making a move from one state of affairs to another is perfectly normal and reasonable. But having Anxiety to the extent where we avoid making any changes, no matter how desirable the end result might be, is a problem that needs addressing. I have included a separate section on Anxiety in Part Two of this book. If this is a problem for you then hopefully that section will help you understand a lot more about what Anxiety is and how it can be managed.

Next, research any key skills you might need to gain and any critical timings you might need to be aware of. This is where we start to refine the key events that need to happen for us to reach our goal(s). We might also need to learn some new skills, or even go back to school or college and get some qualifications. If we need to study we will need to find out what qualification is necessary. Be warned that there are some bogus qualifications out there, or qualifications that will not allow you to do what you want to do. For example, if you want to teach Yoga, Mindfulness, become a counsellor, or therapist make sure that you check with someone who is already doing the job. It is unlikely that a couple of days, or a couple of weeks will be enough to become a 'professional' skilled person. I have seen some sad examples of where people have been caught out and worked hard to gain worthless qualifications.

Draw up a critical path. The things that must happen for you to get to where you want to get to. This is where you start to put things in order – in the right order. I need to do X before Y. I can only do X each October and I need to book it up three months beforehand etc. Therefore I need to book up X before the end of July and as X takes 6 months to complete, I won't be able to move on to the next stage until next April. If I miss the July timeframe I could be delayed by 12 months etc.

Draw all this up and see how it looks. This is a route map of your journey. How congruent is it overall? What are the tough spots? How congruent are you at each of the different stages? You can move back to our river analogy and draw this up as if it were a flowing river. Almost like a continuation of your Life Audit (if you chose to draw it that way). Work through this route map a few times and gradually add more detail. Also, take the opportunity to revisit your objectives. Re-read your letter from the future. Go further back in the process and test out different parts of your journey using techniques such as the 'Day in the Life'. You will then be at a point where you can move to the next stage of considering what you need to actually do each day in order to make it happen.

But before you move on to the next stage, you might have already noticed that there is a massive advantage to planning your journey the way that you have. Most of us know that life doesn't always run smoothly. Things happen that really are outside of our control. This might be illness (our own or a close friend or relative). It could be financial. The days of 'a job for life' seem like a distant memory now, and people can, and do, lose their jobs through no fault of their own. I don't want to be too negative, and I am not going to simply list out all the things that can go wrong. So here is the advantage of planning your journey the way that we just have. Because you have turned the destination into a journey and checked for congruency throughout your plan, you have already made it as resilient as you can against a lot of the unforeseen problems that can happen. If you have to stop and pause things for a while, you are already somewhere along a path that is a congruent one, where what you are doing matches your values. Maybe not 10/10 yet, but at the very least, congruency has been built into the process. And because you have already considered alternatives and possible places to stop off. Remember the 'sailing days of yore' analogy that we started with. Olden day sailors considered that they were are sailing towards a destination rather than to one. They had plenty of alternative ports to stop off at where they could sit out the storm. If you do have to postpone your plans for a while, better to do it in a place that is already under your control and aligned with what you want to do with your life.

What do I need to do today?

As I noted earlier, there are two absolutely key timeframes we need to always bear in mind. The first is 'our lifetime', the second is 'today'. At this point, we have considered our lifetime a lot; what we want to do with our one life. Now let's turn our attention to the second key timeframe, 'today'. Today is the time period when we actually do things and make the changes that will get us to where we want to be.

Let's take an example. I am currently sitting in the South of England as I write this. If I decided that I wanted to cycle to the South of Italy and wanted to get there around the end of next summer, I could draw up a rough plan very quickly. I could estimate the number of miles (or Kilometres – which is what they use in Italy). I could work out an average distance I could cycle per day. I also know I need to get across (or under) the Channel (the bit of sea between England and France), and then go sort of South East towards the top of Italy, and then travel mostly South. However, If I get to the end of my driveway on day one and don't know whether I need to turn right or left, and if I do something similar to this every single day, I am probably not going to meet my overall plan of getting to where I want to be in the timeframe I have set. Sure, it's OK to get lost once or twice and learn from this. But knowing what to do today is vital. Otherwise I am just getting on my bike and riding in a random direction.

Our plan will give us a good overall idea of the main things I need to do and by when. Write out all the key dates – on a large sheet of paper or a calendar. Work out any lead times. Figure out how much time you might need to devote to each one. If it involves learning a new skill like a musical instrument, language or craft then you will probably need to practice each and every day. Do some research. There are some good guides out there that can help you with these type of tasks. For example imagine you wanted to run in some sort of fun run in several months time. There are guides that can tell you exactly what you need to do on a daily basis to get from zero running experience right up to completing a marathon (or 5K, 10K, half-marathon etc). Such plans will both tell you what you need to do each day and how long it will take you overall. Your key milestones will already give you an indication of the main things you will need to achieve and they might have timeframes associated with them. There will almost certainly be a natural order in which you should approach them. Each of these can be broken down into a number of smaller steps and milestones, and these smaller steps will ultimately become a set of individual tasks that will need to be done on a specific day.

Go back to your Letter from the Future. The one you wrote when you were formulating your goals and objectives. Remember that the letter is from 'me' to 'me' and written from a point in time as if I had already got to the point where I wanted to be. What we are going to do now is to expand our letter and not just describe what we are doing 'now' that we have arrived at our preferred future. We will also say what we did to get here.

So, with apologies to those of you who were reaching for your seasickness pills when I wrote my own letter from the future from the Scottish loch, I will continue with that example. You may remember that I finished the letter by thanking myself for making the decision I did to choose this life. The next step from is to tell yourself (from the future) what it was you did to make this happen. The powerful thing about this is that you are describing what you did from a position where you have already succeeded. You are writing from a position when it has already happened. This is much more powerful than telling yourself what you need to do in order to make it happen.

Imagine for a moment that in order to reach your preferred future you will need to learn a specific new skill that requires consistent and regular study or practice. There are many example of this, learning a new language, a musical instrument, a craft of some sort (carpentry, dressmaking, water painting), tap dancing, ice-skating, fire juggling – the list is endless. It is very easy to consider that if we want to learn to speak French it might take us six of twelve months to become proficient and that it is important for us to study and practice every day. We should listen to our audio course every single day, press the pause button and respond to the prompts etc. We might also need to memorise a number of new words each day. So I might say to myself that in order to learn French over the next twelve months I need to do all these things. That is true, but not very powerful. A way to really make sure that I do this is to imagine myself at a point in the future (say twelve months away) where I am actually speaking fluent French and enjoying the fruits of my efforts. I can then tell myself what it is I did to get to this point. "I can speak fluent French because every day over the last twelve months I made sure

I spent at least 30 minutes working through my X. Y, Z course". "I never missed a single day". This approach is powerful because I am writing from the powerful position of success; I can already feel what it is like to have succeeded. My effort has already paid off. All the hard work was worth it. Even doing this in an imaginary way fires off a very different and more positive set of emotions which are based on having accomplished something. If you start to procrastinate, lose motivation, or get stuck, pull out your letter from the future and re-read it.

So the sort of thing I might include at the end of my 'Scottish loch' letter might be along the lines of.

"…

I am so glad that I chose to do this with my life and I wanted to write and thank you for making this all possible. The work you put in really paid off.

The way I got to where I am now was:

- I always wrote my plans and tasks in my planning diary, and I stuck to what I had written.
- I reviewed progress every week on a Sunday evening at 8 pm. I checked against my congruency alignment and reviewed any upcoming milestones and critical dates. I wrote a brief weekly plan based on this.
- I wrote a to-do list every evening based on my weekly plan at about 9 pm each evening and transferred specific tasks into the dated part of my diary.
- I always did the tasks on my daily to-do list and ticked them off in my diary.
- I kept a spreadsheet of forecast and actual spending and made sure that I did not overspend even if this meant extending timescales. I always double

checked that my finances worked both on paper and in reality.

- I saved money and developed alternative (passive) income streams through writing which enabled me to be able to 'retire' and sail off four years earlier than my statutory retirement age.
- I downsized my possessions and lived on a small sailboat in a marina for 12 months to double check if this really was a life I could enjoy. It was, I loved it.
- I studied and passed all my sailing qualifications.
- I looked at my planning diary every single morning (I still do) and checked that I was 'exactly where I wanted to be and doing exactly what I wanted to be doing'.

I am now living the life of a £200 millionaire and am so pleased that I put in the effort to actually make it all happen. I am proud of myself. It was 100% worth it.

Very Best Wishes

From me"

The key with this letter from the future is to put yourself into a pretend time machine and really imagine yourself in that successful place where you have achieved your preferred future. Then look back and figure out what it was that made the difference and really helped you to get to where you are; what were the non-negotiable things that mean the difference between succeeding and failing? Your letter might be a lot shorter than my Scottish loch one. For example:

"Dear me

I am so pleased that I can now play the piano and sing all the popular songbook tunes that people love. Last night I played to a restaurant full of people celebrating their friends' 25th anniversary. They were so pleased that I got my fee and a generous tip as well as two future bookings.

I got to this point by working hard over the last two years. I practiced at least 30 minutes every single day and longer at weekends. After the first year I set a target to learn one new song by heart each week. I never missed a practice and it was so worth the other sacrifices I made to do this. I even taped a large sign to the TV screen saying 'only watch if you have done your 30 minutes practice today.'

I am proud of myself and all that I have done to get here.

All the very best

From me"

One of the key things that should be evident in your letter is that in order to succeed, you needed to make a plan, keep it under review and make sure you actually did your daily tasks – whether the task was a regular one that had to be done every day like piano practice, or a one-off that needed to be scheduled in, like doing an internet search of how to qualify as a driving instructor.

The key Aphorism to be very aware of at this point is:

"It doesn't matter if I do it today or tomorrow. It matters if I do it today"

We will look at this in detail in the next section (Aphorisms and how to use them). It is so important. What we need is a useful way to help us to make things happen; to make sure we do what we need to today. What we require is a mechanism or tool to make sure that we don't leave things vague and hanging in space, "well I'll do it sometime during the next week...."

The following is what I recommend. You must get yourself some form of planning diary; sometimes called a notebook diary. This should include a space with the days written in where we can add appointments, events, daily to-do lists etc. And some space where we can do some planning. My preferred format is a ring binder (easier to fold out flat) and quite large (A4 in the UK, Quarto in the USA). Having a week-to-view is also good as this allows us an overview of the next and past few days, but also gives us enough space to focus on today. I like the format where you have the days of the week on one side and an empty page for notes on the facing page.

So we now have our tool, how do we use it? Once you have an overall view of your plan start to transfer the key dates into your planning diary. These might be things like, college enrolment day, the cut-off to book stall at craft fair, presentations or talks that might be informative, or anything else where there is a specific date that can't be changed. You should also include other more standard important dates such as Insurance Renewal, birthdays, Holiday, In-laws visiting etc. You can also write a few things in the notes pages, for example a broad brush type of statement as to where you would like to be, "This is May, my plan is to have written to all the volunteer organisations in a 20 mile radius and see if…." The point is to include as much from your plan as you can. Get it onto paper; words, diagrams, cartoons, whatever suits you best. You might need to guess a bit at where and when you might include things in the notes. You can review your planning diary at any time and add to it or make changes.

You will then need to book two key recurring appointments with yourself in the diary. The first is a weekly meeting with yourself. Normally no more than 20 minutes or half an hour. Choose a regular time and day slot that is a good thinking time for you. I like a Sunday morning or evening, you might prefer some completely different time. But make sure that you can be focused and undisturbed. The objective of this weekly meeting is to review how things went last week and decide what needs to happen next week. At its most simple, just write a to-do list of things that need to be accomplished next week. Write this on the notes page. Then have a look at this list and see if there are things that have to be done on a particular day of that week. Either put a check, tick or cross against that item (or a line through it) and transfer it to the day it needs to be done. You are effectively building up a 'what do I need to do today' daily to-do list from your weekly list. You can of course put items into different weeks in the future if that is more relevant. When you get to that week and have your weekly meeting you can then allocate the items/tasks to specific days.

The second reoccurring appointment with yourself is a daily one. This is done towards the end of each day. You choose the best time based on your energy levels. Probably no more than 10 minutes. This is where you quickly review how today went, crossing off or checking/ticking the items from today's to-do list (you can of course cross them off as you go, but still review them at the end of the day), and then confirm your to-do list for tomorrow. This will probably also involve crossing off items from the weekly to-do list and putting them into the daily one.

Let's take a very simple example of how this might work, and I have included a simple diagram below to illustrate this. One of the things that many people consider is the possibility of either downsizing or minimalizing their lives in order to reduce overheads. We do tend to hang on to a lot of things as we move through our lives and sometimes having so many things can literally take up so much physical space that we literally become stuck. Imagine that we have gradually filled our garage with

114

'stuff' over the years (possibly including the Abs machine from earlier) and now we have a garage packed with things we had accumulated that just sit there. However, having that garage space would really help us in moving towards our Preferred Future. Maybe we need it for storage space for products to do with our new business, a workshop, a music room, a weaving loom, a home gym (maybe we will actually get to use the Abs machine), or even (and this literally never happens in the UK at least) a car. Clearing a

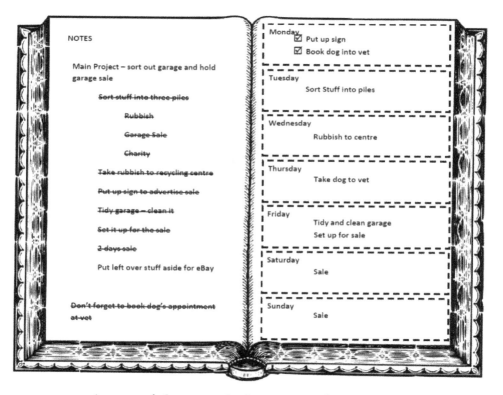

garage is one of those typical manyana/tomorrow types of tasks that simply never gets done, "it's trivial, I can do it anytime", or "It's a monster task I just don't have time now, I'll do it sometime later". What we can do by using the planning diary approach I am about to explain is decide on a specific week when we will get it done. On Sunday when we have our weekly planning meeting with ourselves we can note down the key activities on the notes page of our planning diary (the page opposite the dated days of that week). Example tasks might be; Sort stuff into piles for recycling, giving to charity, or selling at a garage sale. We would need to actually run the garage sale, possibly over the weekend. Of course we will also need to tidy up the garage and make it presentable for the sale. Oh, and mustn't forget to actually take the 'rubbish' to the recycling centre. Anything else? Oh, I had better advertise the garage sale, maybe put a sign up so people will know in advance to come along. And if things don't get sold, maybe I can put them on ebay or Craigslist etc. Oh, nearly forgot, I need to take the dog to the vet to get his jabs sometime that week as well.

Once you have written these tasks down on the notes page you can start to transfer them onto a specific day. So, 'Put up sign to advertise sale' and 'Book dog into vet' would probably get written into Monday. We then put a line through these items on the notes page to acknowledge that they are now assigned to a specific day. I can write the days for the actual garage sale in as well as I know that this will happen on Saturday and Sunday and put a line through them on the notes page. However, I might be unsure at the moment as to when I do the other things as they need to fit in around the dog's vet appointment (top priority). When Monday comes I know 'What I need to do Today' and I do it (put up the sign and book the dog's appointment). I tick (check) these two items. I have booked the dog in for Thursday, so I write this in to that day as a task. When I have my daily meeting with myself I can then go ahead and transfer all the other tasks to their appropriate days. So, on Tuesday I know that I need to sort the stuff in the garage into three different piles. And so it goes on etc. I might not allocate everything. For example I don't know if I will need to put anything on ebay; I might sell the lot during the garage sale. I won't know until late on Sunday afternoon what is left over. If I sell everything I can simply strike this through. If I don't, I can transfer it to the notes page for the next week and start to plan accordingly; take photographs, prepare packaging material, write descriptions etc.

You might be thinking that this is a painstakingly obvious example that really doesn't need this much detail or explanation. After all, anyone can organise and carry out a garage sale without any need to do anything else other than have a quick think about it. Well, true. But what this method does is two things. Firstly, it can help you deal with a multitude of different tasks, projects and sub-projects at the same time. It can help you to prioritise and schedule what needs to happen first. You don't want to get to Saturday before remembering that the signs need to go up. Secondly, it requires you to commit to what you need to do Today. It makes you allocate specific tasks to specific days. This method is a great tool to both keep you on track and also avoid procrastination. And when you have your weekly meeting with yourself, you don't have to restrict yourself to just writing things in the notes page for the coming week. If the dog needs a booster injection in three months' time, then write that into the appropriate notes page. If you know that there is a street festival on a particular day that you want to go to, write it in – and don't forget to make a note a few weeks earlier reminding you to make yourself a costume.

You can start practicing this now, even before you have fully decided on what your preferred future is going to be. Simply use this method for your day-to-day planning. And, of course, you can use it for planning the process of deciding what you want to do with your one life as you work your way through this book. A bonus effect is that you will find that once you have written tasks down in this manner, you no longer need to keep things spinning round in your head and it gives you more time to focus on more important things – like what to do with your one life.

Of course, you could also decide that you need a monthly meeting with yourself which you would use to define your key objectives and tasks for the next month which are then put into weekly lists in your planning diary. And depending on the length or complexity of your overall plans, you might even have a quarterly or even yearly planning session. In fact many of us do have a sort of yearly planning session. We call this our New Year resolutions. They normally get written down on 1st January and are forgotten about by the start of February. I hope you can see that the processes being described up to this point are very different from this. Although, it is possible that you have bought this book in January precisely to help you with deciding on, and sticking to, your New Year resolutions. If that is the case, then excellent, I hope you find that the methods and suggestions in this book really bring those resolutions to life – but you will check that your resolutions are congruent, won't you?

This process might all sound a bit mechanical. In a way it is, but there are several advantages to doing things this way:

- Writing a daily to-do list the night before is a great way of getting a good night's sleep. Once the things we need to do tomorrow are written down our brain can decide do stop worrying about them. To stop worrying that we might forget them. We can say to ourselves "It's OK, it's on the list. I don't need to think about that now"
- Having the plan in a planning diary means that we have one master copy of both the plan and the activities. And having it in an actual physical diary gets it out there and into the real world, actual ink on paper, and it is in the real world where the changes will happen that will get you to where you want to be.
- It is a great way of tracking accomplishments. You will literally have a record of all the great things you have done to get to where you want to be. Your planning diary will become the second part of the Letter from the Future. "I got here because....{I did all the things in my planning diary}"

Maintaining the Plan

This is where we check that we are still on track with regard to being congruent with our life values. It is possible to drift without knowing it. Or maybe working through the plan has highlighted some problems with the original plan that we didn't recognise at the time.

Let's take the example of Bernard Moitessier. You may, or may not, not have heard of him. He was a world renowned and eminent single-handed sailor. He was famously leading the 1968 Sunday Times Golden Globe Race after several months at sea. This was the first single-handed round the world yacht race. The prize was to be awarded for the fastest time. Moitessier was clearly in the lead well into the race and was about to head back up to the start/finish line in Plymouth, England. He had already been round the infamous Southern Ocean and rounded the equally infamous Cape Horn. Then, crossing the Atlantic, he decided not to head North to the finish line but to round The Cape of Good Hope in South Africa for a second time then, also for a second time, pass Australia and New Zealand and head for Tahiti. He was effectively abandoning the race but then continuing to sail for a farther distance than it would have been to head North for the finish line in Plymouth. So why did he do this? His brief explanation was given in a message he sent by slingshot to a passing boat (this was the 1960's remember –

communication at sea was very basic). His message, which was an explanation to the London Times newspaper, simply said, "…because I am happy at sea and perhaps to save my soul". Having read his book of the voyage (The Long Way) it is clear that Moitessier was dealing with who he was and what he believed in as much as where he was going. It seems to me that the idea of winning a commercial long distance sailing race was not in tune with who he was and why he sailed. Crossing an arbitrary line for the purpose of winning was not in line with his life values. Continuing in the race would not have been congruent for him. So the moral of this story? I guess it is never too late to check for congruence even if you are 80% toward where you think you want to be. You might get there and find it was the wrong destination. Moitessier literally discovered that his journey really was his destination.

This also seems like a good point to provide a bit of an explanation as to why the mountaineers Brand and Brown (remember them?) decided not to set food on the actual summit of Kangchenjunga. This is very simple really, and you have probably guessed it. The summit, the very top part, of the mountain is deemed sacred by the people of Sikkim. Brand and Brown made a promise that they would respect the sanctity of the top of the mountain, and they kept to that promise as have all the subsequent climbers to this day. This tradition has continued as much as a respect for Brand and Brown as it has for the respect of the Sikkim people. It is worth always bearing in mind that as you strive to achieve your preferred future, there is no excuse to trample on the sacred ground of someone else's life and beliefs, "If you can't be the sun, don't be a cloud".

Nine things to do

1. Buy a planning dairy
2. Schedule a weekly review time in your diary. Decide on a time and day that is good for you. Possibly a Saturday morning or a Sunday evening – do what is best for you and stick to it.
3. Formulate your goals. Describe what you will be doing in the future when you have arrived there. Be descriptive, positive and vivid. Do this as a letter from the future, or possibly a video from the future (you talking to you).
4. Draw up a 'river' plan. Get a large sheet of paper and draw up the path (or different paths) that can get you to where you want to be. Draw the milestones as bends in the river. These might be a couple of tricky bits with rapids, waterfalls or even crocodiles. There might also be a few locations where you would be happy to linger for a while.
5. Do a congruency alignment check. Which bits of my journey will be toughest, which the most congruent? Scale these aspects from 0-10. Write the numbers on your river plan.
6. Transfer 'fixed' and important dates into your planning diary. Check reality against your critical path.

7. Finish the Letter/Video from the Future. "I got to where I am because I did X. Y and Z

8. Start living as much of your preferred future as possible right now – you might be surprised at what you can already do.

9. Make a contract with yourself that you will do this and stick to it. Or even stick it on the TV, or somewhere else relevant that you can't ignore.

Aphorisms – and how to use them

First off. What is an aphorism? Well, generally an aphorism is a short pithy statement that contains some self-evident general truth about life, or how to live it. Aphorisms are normally quite astute and memorable, and often a bit quirky. Some are much too saccharine sweet and sentimental – for my taste anyway. Some appear to give an insight into the meaning of life itself. A lot of families have their own aphorisms which are passed on down the generations. You probably have a few favourites of your own. Most burn brightly whilst we read them and are then forgotten…forever. So, not particularly useful, and this book is all about being useful.

But I do quite like aphorisms. They can be "useful" if used correctly. They can be very valuable motivational tools that can help us when things get tough, to get us out of a rut, or to remind us why we are doing what we are doing. I have included a few that I have picked up over the years. A bit like the 'Things to Do' lists at the end of the previous sections I have kept the suggested Aphorisms down to about 9 (depending on how you count them). Any more than that and they will start to become unmanageable and lose some of their impact. Some you will have heard before, some I have made up, some you may like and some you may hate. I would encourage you to collect and make up some of your own. The general rule is simple; if one works, use it, if it doesn't, then don't – but try and find one that does. Also, don't choose too many at any one time. Between 3 and 6 is probably plenty. Swap them around, some might be more relevant at different stages of your journey. And of course; they are only useful if you use them. This section does not contain too much 'new' information as such. Although there is quite a bit more detail on ensuring that your plan is financially sound. I left this until a bit later as it is so easy to get completely hung up too early on this aspect and wrongly start putting ideas onto the CANNOT list when they really shouldn't be. These Aphorisms are here to 'glue' some of the previous idea together and provide you with tools that are based on the concepts contained in the book. They are broadly in the same order that these ideas were originally presented. Aphorisms can be extremely useful tools that actually provide the push to either get you going or keep you going. They are a great antidote for procrastination.

I am going to go into a bit of detail on each one of the aphorisms that follow. I have found that simply repeating the words like some form of mantra does not work; because if you just repeat it then nothing changes; nothing is put into action.

Having said that, there has been some fascinating research into one of the best known 'aphorisms' of all time, "Every day, in every way, I am getting better and better". It originated from the French psychologist Emile Coue who pioneered self-improvement through 'optimistic autosuggestion'. The idea was that through repeating this mantra up to 20 times a day and without doing anything else, you could 'cure' yourself of certain troubles that had a basis in unconscious thought. There is conflicting evidence on whether or how this mantra might work. Some say it does and some say it doesn't. I will stick with Aphorisms that are rooted in the idea on making us change our behaviour in a motivational way in order to achieve our preferred future.

My take on this is that to work an Aphorism should jolt the brain a bit. Somewhat like splashing a cupped handful of cold water into your face. It is vital that there is something of a brain jolt as one of the key uses of the Aphorisms below is to stop us drifting back into…well…drifting. They are used to remind us of what we need to do and why we need to do it – the bridge between simply thinking something and actually doing it. Hence, as you will see below, an Aphorism can be, and maybe should be, slightly illogical but at the same time compelling. It is the 'jolt' that wakes us up and spurs us into action. Some Aphorisms do not jolt by being illogical – they are simply fundamental truths that we should bear in mind; a statement of the blindingly obvious.

Let's start off with some Aphorisms that are geared mainly towards the 'what do I want to do?' part of our journey.

So here is the absolutely key Aphorism taking on the form of a question to ask ourselves that we have met right from page one.

"Imagine you only had one life. What would you do with it?"

This was really the starting point for me developing my views on how to live a congruent, fulfilling life and is the Aphorism that has spurred me on to write this book. We really don't have an infinite number of lives that we can keep running through until we find one that we like.

126

We just have the one, so we should make the most of it. A lot of us, myself included, have spent most of our lives simply drifting along with the current and passively accepting whatever life happens to throw at us, good or bad. We put things off and act as if we had all the time in the world to get to where we really want to be; wherever that is. The truth is, we do only have one life and if we don't do the things we want during our lifetime, we never will. Now I don't want to tread on any religious or spiritual belief systems here. But even the most religious or spiritual people I know do acknowledge that what we do during the 'fleeting' time we spend as sentient beings on this earth is important whatever happens afterwards.

This aphorism doesn't simply state that 'you only have one life'. That is a simple truism, but it doesn't really encourage us to do anything to consider changing our ways. An alternative could be, "if you only had one life, what would you do with it?" This immediately moves into the realm of quirkiness – what a daft question. What do you mean "if"? Of course we only have one life, there is no "if" about it. It might move us out of our drifting complacency for a few minutes, but again does not really encourage us to consider starting making any changes. We need more of a Brain Jolt for that.

The word "Imagine" at the start of the aphorism provides the power and movement needed. This is a direct command. You are being told to conjure up this concept of having just the one life. How precious is that, just having one life – can you imagine that? Human imagination is extremely powerful. It is possibly the thing that differentiates us from all (most?) other living creatures. It is the thing that enables us to synthesise different bits of information and solve problems. The development of

127

imagination is part of normal human development and starts very early in childhood. At first all we have are our perceptions; what we see, hear and feel in the world. We store these as memories. We then start using these memories in play. We might play making a cup of tea using toy or real cups. We are playing back events that we have observed. We then move on to weaving different memories and observed events together. A toy boat can become an airplane, or we can invent new creatures by combining different characteristics of other animals. We then start to use symbolism and can easily pretend one object is another. A box can become a castle, a house, a cave, a car, etc – the possibilities are endless; ask any parent who has bought their child an expensive present only to find that the child then spends the rest of the day ignoring the present and playing with the box. We then start to move into the world of fantasy and can imagine things that are outside of our experience, we can imagine what it would be like to predict the future, or be a mermaid, or a Martian. As we get a bit older we can start to conceptualise and have more abstract thoughts. These are things that are not concrete or experienced at all. We can imagine what it might be like to have a soul and what might happen to it after we have died. We can consider complex ethical questions. Because imagination develops naturally as we grow up we don't even think about it, or the fact that we use it all the time. However, as we grow older we often don't exercise our imaginations and start to waste this fabulous resource. Even the most solid of scientific theories ultimately start from the imagination of someone thinking, "Imagine..."

It is said that Einstein came up with the Theory of Relativity from the starting point of asking himself a strange and quirky question, "Imagine I could see forever; what would I see?" He let his imagination loose and suddenly got an image of the back of his head in his mind. So, if he could see 'forever', he would see the back of his head. Now don't ask me how he got from this to physics theories about relativity that I really do not understand. But the point is that the starting point for him was based on a question asking himself to really dig into his powers of imagination.

Your imagination is not something to be wasted. It is a powerful resource. You should use it. Many of us underestimate our powers of imagination. We say things to ourselves like, "but I'm not a creative person, I don't have a good imagination". That is simply not true; it really isn't. We actually use our imagination every day. The simple act of deciding what to do today is based on drawing pictures in our mind of possible scenarios and alternatives. We are creating possibilities that don't exist in the real world at the moment (they are in the future) and then making decisions based on how we consider these possibilities. When I talk about a 'Preferred Future' this is simply likewise using our imagination to draw up a picture of the life we would like to lead. There are plenty of suggestions in the first part of this book such as using the Miracle Question to help you to figure out what that preferred future might look (and feel, and sound) like. This first Aphorism is a powerful one. It is good as a starting point and equally good as a motivator once you start off on your journey.

So, again, still in the realms of the 'what do I want to do?" part of our quest, here is one that I particularly like.

"If you don't know where you are going, that is exactly where you will end up."

or

"If I don't know where I am going, that is exactly where I will end up."

You can say a lot of these aphorisms using "you" or "I". Sometimes it is good to personalise it as "I" – coming from within yourself. Sometimes it is good to be an external you (like a best friend being objective and encouraging you) and use "you". Try both, and try saying them out loud whenever possible – it will feel a bit strange at first.

What? This one doesn't make sense either, but it does give us a Brain Jolt as we try and figure it out – and then the sense of it hits us. Where is it exactly that we will end up? Nowhere or Anywhere? Well that is the whole point of this aphorism. We don't know where. It could be anywhere, it could be no-where. It could be right where we are now. And by the way, staying where we are right now is fine. But only if I have done all my designing and imagining of a preferred future etc. But if I allow myself to be like a rudderless origami boat in a stream it may not take much to knock me out from where I am and send me off to somewhere random.

This aphorism is useful to say to yourself from time to time. Sometimes you might start to feel a bit lost or overwhelmed on your journey. Sometimes you might get into a comfortable place and stop considering "what I need to do today". Sometimes you might do this for a few days, or weeks, or years. It is a good idea to just pull yourself up occasionally and check that you are doing the steering and not just drifting towards somewhere, anywhere, or nowhere.

Consider these two statements:

"Ready, aim, fire"

and

"Ready, fire, aim"

If you were an Olympic archery coach, which one would you be recommending for your athletes? Obviously the first one. But in archery the target is so obvious. It is usually a round thing with circles, and the nearer we get to the middle one the better we will score and the more chance we have of carrying off a gold medal. In life we sometimes act as if our 'target' was as obvious as that of the archer. Yes, well obviously what I want is a big house, a new car, 2.4 children, a holiday each year, promotion at work and a gold credit card. Actually, we don't usually say, "well obviously..." We simply take a lot of these things as read, as givens. We might ponder the details a bit. Do I want a BMW or a Mercedes, a swimming pool or a tennis court, a helicopter or a yacht? Make sure you aim before you fire, and make sure you are aiming at the right thing. Anyone could pretend to be a good archer if they went and drew circles round their arrows after they had landed.

"Getting what I want is easy, deciding what I want is difficult"

This might sound a bit bland. It doesn't give a big jolt. It also sounds patently untrue. We have been told all our lives to focus on the difficult bit of actually striving and working hard to get something. However, as I have discussed many times, if we don't really cover the fundamentals and figure out what it is we are striving for – then why are we striving at all? I once had a wise manager who encouraged his team to really figure out what the objective of the work task was. He wanted us to be smart and really think about our SMART goals rather than simply being busy. His Aphorism was that, "Anyone can be a busy idiot". Have you ever had the situation in an exam where you are so wound up after all your revision and the time pressure of the exam itself that you quickly read the question and then start furiously writing everything you know on the subject? The only problem is that you haven't read the question carefully enough and, although everything you are writing is correct, it doesn't really answer the actual question written on the exam paper. Actually slowing down and really understanding what it is you are being asked is at least as hard (I would argue harder) than answering it. And by focusing on answering what is being asked, you will get more marks. So this Aphorism is telling us, or reminding us, that we should not skip over what we always seem to think is the easy or obvious part.

How about a different version of this? I like this one.

"Getting a million is easy, deciding what to spend it on is difficult"

Is this true? It seems to be the opposite. Surely deciding that I want to be a millionaire is the easy part and becoming a millionaire is the part that is more difficult. Well, getting a million may be as simple as buying a lottery ticked that happens to be a winning one. We discussed earlier in this book about how difficult it is to really decide what you would spend your lottery winning on and the fact that in reality for many people winning the lottery does not bring them happiness or long term satisfaction

132

and a fulfilled life. So, think about it, if you are unlikely to become fulfilled and happy after the effortless task of being lucky enough to purchase a winning lottery ticket, why do you think you would be any more fulfilled and happy if you work hard all your life focusing solely on getting a million saved in the bank to spend when you stop?

You have probably read a few biographical books, or heard a few stories, of people who have realised for some reason that they had been striving for most of their lives for something they didn't really ever want in the first place. Hopefully they have realised this 'before it is too late'. Although I would argue that it is never too late. I suppose that if your goal in life was to write a book about how you spend most of your life doing the wrong thing before discovering this when it was nearly too late, then fair enough. But I doubt that anyone actually sets off with that goal in mind.

But what if I fundamentally believe that my goal really is to become a millionaire? My thinking might be that if I can get to £1 million (or $1 million), I can then make whatever choices I want. I could turn my life into a perpetual holiday. But to get to that point I need to sacrifice everything else and just focus on getting my million. There are people who do this, or a close version of it, and that is fine if it really is your choice. But it certainly doesn't fit in with the idea of living a congruent life where the journey and the destination are the same thing. And remember the comment at the end of the section on planning. If something goes wrong and we get interrupted in the middle of an incongruent plan, we have no safe harbours to stop off at and our life becomes very incongruent and unhappy. This might have even been what happened to you and was the reason you picked up this book.

I read a very inspirational short story a few years ago called, "The £200 millionaire" by Weston Martyr. It was written in 1932, so to bring things up to today's prices we should really rename it "The £10,000 millionaire". Weston Martyr recounts a story of a hard working professional couple on their much valued annual holiday. Their passion was sailing and they chartered a decent sized sailing boat for two weeks each year. Their dream was to eventually retire, buy their own small yacht and sail off into the sunset. In order to do this they 'knew' that they needed to amass quite a lot of funds and savings. But it would be worth it. One year on their travels they met up with a retired doctor when he tied his boat up next to theirs. He was in his late 60's but had retired over ten years earlier having sold his London practice and moved to the East Coast of England. He had worked hard all his life, but unfortunately lost his wife, and his children had moved out and were self-sufficient. He discovered that there was no one left to work for. He was disinterested in his work and feeling very tired. But unfortunately retirement didn't suit him. "…I soon found out that having nothing to do at all is even worse than working hard at something you've lost interest in." Almost by chance he hired a small sailing boat and stayed on it cruising local waters for a month. A seed was planted and he started to wonder if he could buy his own boat and do this full time, sailing down to the South of Europe for the colder months. There is a very interesting description in the story showing how he calculated how he thought he could manage on his small income of £200 per year (interest on the capital he had saved). He didn't have a Spreadsheet in 1932, but did carefully work out his anticipated costs on paper (You will meet a pair of Aphorisms explaining why this is important in a few pages). He then made the jump, bought a boat and never regretted his decision. He toured all over the Canal systems in France, Germany, Holland and Switzerland (By the way, if you are reading this in the USA or Canada you could translate this easily into the Intracoastal Waterway, The Great Lakes, Hudson and Erie Canal etc). Interestingly he described his move as a very small step rather than a big jump, but it completely changed his life. He was living the life of a millionaire on £200 a year (As I say, approximately £10,000 in today's money). What is more he had, on average, £40 left over each year. As Dickens would have said, "Result, Happiness."

One of the things I really like about this story is the way Weston Martyr describes the congruence of this £200 millionaire lifestyle. He describes a physical and mental transformation from someone who had pretty much given up on life, to someone who is truly living a meaningful life in full accord with his values and beliefs. You can almost imagine the two circles of 'who I am' and 'what I do' moving together to become one as he takes the small step into a new (preferred) future. Of course as our £200 hero is describing all this to the couple they can't help but start wondering if this would be possible for themselves. And, actually, they figure out that it could be. They are both writers and could write just as easily from a small sailboat travelling around Europe as they could from their small flat. And this was in the days long before the internet.

So the 'hero' in Weston Martyr's book didn't actually need to either win a million or have a million in order to live his millionaire life. He simply needed to be congruent and have slightly more money left over each month than he spent. The book (also called 'The £200 Millionaire') this short story is taken from is now long out of print.

However, it has been reprinted and reproduced on may blogs and websites and can be easily found on the internet if you want to read the original.

Let us now move on to a few more Aphorisms, but this time ones that are more geared towards that part where we have decided what we want to do and we are striving towards actually achieving our preferred future. Here is an Aphorism I have mentioned before and it is a good one to use when things go wrong and we have setbacks that make us feel we are right back where we started.

"Life does is not a game of snakes and ladders."

I am not sure if this really jolts, but it is useful to have this stored away and get used to saying it every time that Negative Automatic Thought pops into our head that we are back to square one.

We can't control everything and we will get knock backs. Some of these might be fairly major. If you look at the example Life Audit in Part Two where I use some of my own experiences as an example you will see that I once had a business knockback which quite literally meant losing everything (money and house etc). It is very easy and natural at these times to feel like we are right back at the beginning and we need to start from the very first step again. In fact a better way of looking at it is that we have come off the rails a bit. We have been knocked to one side. This is where we need to gather our thoughts and strength and pull ourselves back onto the tracks and keep going. We will have amassed a lot of knowledge and experience to get to where we are now. Even if this is a crushing setback, we can use that knowledge and experience to good use and figure out what to do next. There is a bit of a cheeky (tongue in cheek) Aphorism that is related to this one and is in the form of a rule. If you can stick to it, you won't go far wrong.

"There are only two times you should give up. 1) When you have won, or 2) Never"

Let's move on to the next Aphorism. There are times in our lives where we sort of just sit around waiting for something to happen. I quite like the description a critic gave of Samuel Becket's play, "Waiting for Godot". The critic said it was a play where "nothing happened...twice". Doing nothing is not a good option for getting the life you want. Don't let your life become a series of 'nothing happening' several times whilst you are hanging around for something to come along – it most probably won't. There is a short discussion on Procrastination at the end of the section on Anxiety in Part Two. Use the following Aphorism to remind yourself that if you are procrastinating or not moving forward then you really are just drifting again. This is the most boring sounding Aphorism in this book, but possibly one of the most important. Here it is;

"If I don't make it happen, no-one else will"

This is a good one to try with "you" instead of "I". Tell yourself this very firmly and see the difference it makes. The power of this one is it is the simple brutal truth. "If I stop pedalling, I won't get up the hill". Of course when you bring this one to mind you can also turn it round and make it positive. "If I make it happen, it will happen".

Lets us now consider an absolutely vital pair of Aphorisms regarding money. I said right at the beginning that the aim of this book was to be useful. For it to actually be used, and being used means that it must work in reality. And of course there is nothing quite as real as money and the need to have some of it in order to survive. Money has been mentioned a number of times, but mainly in the context of trying to explain why having a lot of money does not (necessarily) buy happiness, and that conversely if you are moving towards living a congruent life then you can possibly do this for a lot less than you think. But having said that, even Weston Martyr didn't call his book, "The £1 millionaire". Most of us do not have an independent income and we need to be able to finance ourselves somehow. We need somewhere to live and food to eat. This next Aphorism is actually a set of two. They are of vital importance and must be taken as a pair;

"If you can't make it work on paper, it won't work in reality"
And
"Just because it works on paper doesn't mean it will work in reality"

I have used these two a lot for financial planning. They really do come as a pair. It is true that we do sometimes need to take a leap of faith and start on our path without all the loose ends being finalised or tidied up. However, there is a big difference between taking a calculated risk and being reckless.

Let's take an example. Imagine that your life dream was to live off-grid in a cabin in the woods. You might have some capital up front to fund this (from savings or an inheritance etc). You might be able to sell an existing property. You might only just be making ends meet at the moment and need to save up for a plot of land, buy building materials and build the cabin yourself. Maybe you could become self-sufficient and your cabin was going to be off-grid so your monthly outgoings were going to be effectively zero. Maybe you could achieve most of this, but let's say you still needed to find £100 a month (or $100 or some other currency) to keep even this minimal lifestyle choice going.

The first part of the Aphorism says that we need to be able to make it work in theory (on paper) before we can commit to trying to make it work in real life. We need to be able to make the numbers add up on paper. Because if they don't, we certainly won't be able to make the real pound notes or dollar bills add up in real life. And this can lead to misery. Remember the quote from Dickens earlier in this book where he defines the difference between happiness and misery. So if you need $100 a month for your cabin in the woods and your income is only £99 – then this simply will not work. You must adjust things to the point where your plan works on paper. Of course by "on paper" I also mean "on a spreadsheet". For those who don't know, a spread sheet is a very powerful computer planning tool that allows you to put rows and columns of numbers as either actual or budget amounts. The magic of computing allows you to do 'what if' type calculations very simply and investigate what happens for different income and expenditure scenarios. Spreadsheets are very powerful and can look quite complicated at first glance. If you have not used spreadsheets before, I would advise seeing if there are any resources (training organisations, patient friends etc) near you who can help you learn the basics. Have a look on the internet. Microsoft's Spreadsheet is called Excel and often comes bundled along with Word and PowerPoint etc. It might already be on your computer. Search for 'Excel for beginners' or similar on YouTube and you will be able to get a good grasp of what spreadsheets can do. Put "learn to use a spreadsheet" into your planning diary and develop your plan of how to do exactly that.

So let us imagine that you have drawn up your financial plan on paper – or on a spreadsheet on your computer. Have I now proved that my plan will now work and I can relax? Unfortunately, not quite. This is where the second part of the aphorism comes in. Our number planning might be excellent and we have worked everything out to the nth degree of accuracy. Yes, I can afford it and I will even have £20 left over every month (my income forecast works out at $120 a month). We relax and look forward to our minimalist lifestyle in the woods. Unfortunately the financial plan on paper is just that; a plan. It is not reality. Reality always has a way of throwing a spanner in the works. Maybe we have made a bad calculation. Maybe the world economy changes or a bad spell of weather might impact on the crops (or herbs or ornaments made from seashells) we are expecting to sell each month. Maybe we need a bit of contingency funding or maybe we haven't fully understood the scope of what we are doing. Watch one of those 'build your own house' TV reality programmes and notice how often there is a massive financial spanner in the works that was unforeseen at the start. For example, the windows being delivered late might have a knock-on effect on the rest of the project that doesn't just mean shifting all the spreadsheet numbers one month to the right. It might mean that the electricians can't start their work, but we still have to pay them or we will lose them and put the whole project at risk. One month of no-windows can mean four months of additional electrician costs.

As I said above, spreadsheets are great, and we can fiddle about with the numbers and do all sorts of 'what if' type analysis to test out different scenarios. However, a particular problem to look out for if we are using a spreadsheet is to start believing that the spreadsheet is reality. It is very tempting to change a few numbers and do a few what-if calculations and then start believing the results. For example, I know that I need an income of £1,000 per month so if I change my spreadsheet so that I; sell 876 cupcakes per month, get 75,432 hits on my YouTube channel, make 47 dog beds a month and sell them all etc....then I will definitely make my £1,000 target. We start to convince ourselves that what we see on paper will happen in reality. This happens more than you might imagine. If your preferred future involves starting up a new business of some sort, or anything else where it is critical to get the numbers right, I would suggest visiting this pair of linked Aphorisms out quite a lot.

The next Aphorism is a good one for challenging procrastination and is back into the realm of giving our brain a jolt;

"It doesn't matter if I do it today or tomorrow, it matters if I do it today"

I love this one it really does give our brains a big jolt as we frown at the logical and grammatical contradiction. It really helps me to stop procrastinating. Again, the power of it is the apparent contradiction of the two parts either side of the comma. However, they are both actually true.

For argument's sake let us imagine that today as you are reading this it is a Monday – and statistically speaking for approximately 1 in 7 of you, it will be. So tomorrow is Tuesday. The fact is that in most cases it probably doesn't matter that I do today's task today (Monday) or tomorrow (Tuesday). However, the word "tomorrow", even when said on a Monday, doesn't really mean "Tuesday" for us most of the time. It means 'Manyana' (which is often used by English speakers to signify 'never' – in the sense of tomorrow never comes). Tomorrow used in this way is that magical unit of time that is always the next day and never actually becomes the present day. It moves on a daily basis as if by magic. If as a child I was asked to tidy my room and my answer was, "I'll do it tomorrow", then both I and my parents know that what I really mean is, "I'm probably not going to do it anytime soon". But when our internal voice says to ourselves, "I'll do it tomorrow", we somehow believe it. I'll go to the gym tomorrow, I'll start my diet tomorrow, I'll do my accounts tomorrow, I'll start learning French tomorrow…ring any bells? It does with me.

So, when we say "tomorrow" to ourselves it does not really mean that specific time period after the next sunrise and before the sunset on the same day. It is simply a way of kicking the can down the street. So, even if it really doesn't matter if I start doing it on Monday or Tuesday, it really does matter that I have started doing it by the end of Tuesday.

"Today" and "Tomorrow" are not equivalent (day) time periods when it comes to putting our plan into action. Today is the fundamental planning period. Tomorrow is simply an excuse to procrastinate. This is one of the reasons why it is so important to have a planning diary as described earlier and make sure that tasks are allocated to actual specific days.

So here comes the final Aphorism in this short series. Remember right back at the start of the book when I asked you to jot down what you would do if you won a fortune on the lottery? Well, consider this for an answer;

"I'm exactly where I want to be, and I'm doing exactly what I want to be doing"

This helps to get us through the tough times, we should always be able to say this. It is also the answer that we should be able to honestly give to the question as to what would I do if I won the lottery. In other words, I'm not waiting for that near impossible dream of winning the lottery, I have decided what I want to do with my one precious life – and if I did perchance happen to win a fortune, I am already doing what I would do (Although I possibly might use the extra cash to get a slight upgrade). If this aphorism isn't a possible answer for you to the lottery question then it is a good time to check your congruence.

However, this Aphorism is also very useful to use when we feel that we are not having a good time and that we are not doing exactly what we want to be doing. We wonder if our current 'pain' is worth it. Maybe at the moment it doesn't feel like it is worth it. This is the time to remind yourself about the congruence of your journey and your destination. I might be working through a plan that will get me to 8/10 congruency. However, at the moment I am going through a temporary phase that is lower than that (say 4/10). I have got into this position knowingly and my letter from the future clearly states that the reason I got to my successful destination (8/10) is partly because I kept

143

going through this difficult (4/10) phase. State this Aphorism quite strongly and quite boldly – out loud if you can. It is the nearest I get to, "Every day in every way I am getting better and better". Because the simple truth is that at this stage if you have truly figured out what you want to do and you are now in the process of getting there, then this Aphorism is by definition true.

Nine Things to do

This is simply a list of the core Aphorisms and a suggestion;

1. Imagine I only had one life what would I do with it?
2. If you don't know where you are going that is exactly where you will end up.
3. Getting what I want is easy, figuring out what I want is difficult
4. Life is not a game of snakes and ladders
5. If I don't make it happen, no-one else will.
6. If I can't make it work on paper it won't work in reality – plus – Just because it works on paper does not mean it will work in reality.
7. It doesn't matter if I do it today or tomorrow, it matters if I do it today.
8. I'm exactly where I want to be and I'm doing exactly what I want to be doing.
9. Take one or two of the above that seem to most fit where you are right now, re-read the descriptions around them and start to fire up your imagination to actually give your brain a jolt and start to put them into practice. Conversely, if you find one that you feel does not help you move forward, then re-read the description around it and make up your own Aphorism that works for you.

Summary of Part One

Right, you have finished reading the main part of this book – possibly for the second time. Now is a good time to sit down, take a breath and have a think about of what you have just read up to this point.

I have drawn what we have been discussing as a diagram. Many people have quite visual imaginations and it can be useful to get things down as a picture on a single page. The diagram represents the journey I have been describing. I think it is good to get an overall picture of the whole process. This is very similar to the idea of increasing our Event Horizon which was discussed right at the start.

You can see the two circles at the top (Who I am &

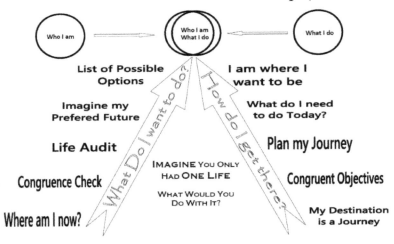

What I do). These move closer to each other as we climb up the two large arrows shaped a bit like a mountain (What do

I want to do? & how do I get there?). The text alongside the two large arrows are some of the key milestones we have been working through as we climbed the mountain and moved from our current situation towards a more congruent fulfilled life where the two circles eventually join and Who I am and What I do become the same thing.

In actual fact, once you have been through these steps on your journey the first time you can always revisit them in any order you like as you refine your ideas. However, initially you should stick to pretty much the order they are presented. Here is a quick description of each:

Where am I now?

We looked at the States of Change model to try and figure out where we might be starting from. Also, we considered that we might be at different stages for different areas of our lives. This is a useful reflective process to understand where we are. It will help you get off to a good start as you start to consider where it is you want to get to.

Congruence Check

This is where we started to consider what is important. What has value for me? What makes my life an authentic one where who I am and what I do are pretty much the same thing? How congruent am I at the moment? This is a key aspect of the whole process as you should always consider your own congruence level both at this early stage and later when you move over to the (How do I get there?) arrow opposite. You can do a congruency check at any point in the process and use it as the key measure of any of the potential preferred futures you start to consider.

Life Audit

This is simply a look at your life this far which is done in a neutral way and can be used to help us clarify our strengths. It can also help to rediscover and re-kindle your previous hopes and dreams that you may have falsely put on to the CANNOT list.

Imagine my Preferred Future

There are many ways to do this including the powerful Miracle Question where you start to really consider what a congruent future might look like. This is where you allow yourself to go beyond just daydreaming and actually start to visualise how things might be different in the future if you were to live the life you choose.

List of Possible Options

At this point you have tried a number of techniques and probably have a number of alternative preferred futures – some very different and some slight variations from each other. You have a good understanding of what living a meaningful life would be and the type of things you could be doing that would make this a reality. You might even have one or many specific options that you wish to follow.

My destination is a journey

This is the start of turning one (or more) of your options into your future reality. At this stage you are making sure that you understand all of your life as 'one life' and do not just focus on some end-point, and disregard the way you get there. We discussed that both your destination and your journey towards it had to be considered as being the same thing. You can't take time-out from your life in order to fulfil your life.

Congruent Objectives

In this section you considered how to describe where you wanted to be in terms that would help you to get there. But at the same time ensuring that you were still being congruent, or at least moving towards congruency. You wrote yourself a letter from the future which described in a vibrant and motivational way what you would be doing and how congruent that would feel for you.

Plan my Journey

Here you started to fill in the gaps and considered the entire task ahead of you. You started to draw up milestones and consider alternatives. You also looked at making sure that your journey means that as you move towards your goal the two circles of Who I am and What I do move closer together. Very importantly you checked that any financial implications of what you are doing will work out in real life. You got yourself a planning diary and started to formalise the details of your plan by writing them down.

What do I need to do Today?

There are two important timeframes, My Lifetime and Today. Today is the unit of time when your plan starts to come to life. It is only what you do today that will make that plan become a reality. You committed your tasks for Today to paper as you implemented your plan and started to see real progress as your preferred future started to become your daily reality.

I am where I want to be

This is the point where you feel that you are living your life the way that you want to be living it. In fact, although this appears at the top of the right hand arrow, it could be anywhere in the process. Once you have started the process and journey of moving towards your preferred future you are no longer like an origami boat drifting aimlessly wherever the current takes you. You are steering your own life in the direction you want to go.

So what now?

Well if this is the first time of reading through this book, continue and read through the next part which covers an example Life Audit and afterwards Anxiety. Then, after a bit of a break to mull things over, start back at page one with some paper, pens and a planning diary, and actually start the process. Work as slowly as you want. Feel free to spend several days, weeks or even months on any of the sections.

Also, if this is your second time of reading through then I hope that you are well on your way to starting your journey towards a more fulfilling and congruent life. I really wish you all the best with it. You might find that you need to revisit some of the sections and re-energise yourself. Do use the Aphorisms, they really can be very powerful.

Most of all, I hope that you have found this book useful and that you have used it. If you have, it would be great if you could just drop a few notes into the review section on Amazon and briefly say what you have found useful and how it made a difference to you. I would love to know what has changed for you as a result of working through it.

PART TWO

Doing a Life Audit

I suggested a number of times in Part One that you try doing a Life Audit once you have read through this book for the first time. Doing a Life Audit is not easy. It is by definition a very personal thing. The idea of an audit as we typically talk about it in a business sense is to have someone independent and objective examine some state of affairs. Being objective about our own life is very difficult. Very often we can be super critical and beat ourselves up over every mistake and wrong decision we have made in the past. This is not helpful. We can't change the past, but we can learn from it. And we can also learn some very positive things about ourselves that may have previously passed us by unnoticed. There is also a risk that we might become very bogged down in psychoanalysing everything that has ever happened to us and try to explain everything we have ever done in terms of some hidden internal psychodynamic psychosocial meanings. In the context of what we are trying to do in this audit, that is also not helpful. What we are trying to do here is to take an objective and detached view on the way our origami boat of a life has floated down the river to this point in time. We simply want to start to understand where we are and how we got to where we are.

A life audit can be written down in words; either prose or bullet points. Or you might prefer to do it in pictorial form. For example you could sketch out an imaginary river snaking its way down the page with notes and drawings of any key events. You could draw in waterfalls, or rocks, or even sharks for the difficult bits. Possibly butterflies, or unicorns, or simply a smiley face emoticon for the good bits. Don't feel you have to do it in chronological order. We actually tend to remember things more based on emotional significance rather than in sequential time sequenced order.

I wanted to provide an example Life Audit. But choosing a fictitious character just to illustrate some of the ideas in this book seemed a little bit less than genuine to me. So I thought that I should use my own life as the example. After all, why should you trust me to ask you to do this if I wasn't prepared to do it myself? Also, you are almost certainly asking who I am to be telling you all this stuff in this book anyway. I would certainly be asking this. It is a very fair question. And of course I am not saying that my life is in any way either typical, radically different, or special. But I have certainly had many different periods where I was drifting and being very incongruent, as well as periods when I managed to accidently become congruent followed by more drifting and finally a very deliberate, and successful, attempt to steer myself in the direction I wanted to go.

So just as an introduction to me, let's kick off with a short section on my basic qualifications and experience relevant to the writing of this book. I will then write out a basic Life Audit of my life path up to this point in order to give you an example of how you might approach your own. I will annotate it with reflections on how it fits in with the ideas from this book, and I would encourage you to do the same. So first let's have the introductory 'qualifications' bit.

I have a number professional qualifications and memberships. At the time of writing (2018) I am a graduate member of the British Psychological Society (BPS), a member of the British Association for Behavioural & Cognitive Psychotherapies (BACP) and am a registered Social Worker. I say, "At the time of writing" as I might well decide to ditch all these things (that is, stop paying the expensive membership subscriptions!) as I move further along my own journey. I have a Bachelor of Science (BSc) degree in Philosophy, Psychology & Sociology, A Masters Degree (MA) in Social Work, and a Postgraduate Diploma (PGdip) in Evidence-Based Psychological Treatment. That last one is a bit of a mouthful. It was basically focused on Cognitive Behavioural Therapy (CBT) and included the audio recording and grading of actual therapeutic sessions – possibly the most demanding qualification I have gained, but well worth the effort for everything I learned.

I have spent the last five years (again writing this in 2018) working in the National Health Service (NHS) in the UK providing mostly one-to-one CBT for individuals with a variety of mental health problems. I have experience of treating most of the Anxiety disorders; Separation Anxiety, Generalised Anxiety Disorder, Social Anxiety, Panic Attacks, Obsessive Compulsive Disorder, Post Traumatic Stress Disorder, and a number of Specific Phobias. I have also worked with Depression, which does tend to go hand-in-hand with Anxiety problems. I have used Solution-Focused Brief Therapy with families and individuals, plus other techniques such as Motivational Interviewing etc. I am also a qualified gym instructor. Shall I stop there? It is starting to sound like I'm showing off. Maybe I am; I hope not. The key thing for me in the context of writing this book has been the discovery that this 'stuff' that I have learnt and used with many people actually works. I have been quite sceptical each time I have approached a new therapeutic, or life-skills, approach. Scepticism can be a very healthy attitude occasionally, but it can also be important to sometimes work through it and try things out for ourselves otherwise we will never know if it will work for us or not. And we remain stuck where we are. I think it is important for you to know that I have only included things in this book that I have seen can work for people. Not everything for everyone works for everybody and not every time, but that really would be asking too much.

The example Life Audit

So, here we go on starting a Life Audit. It is a bit like a very brief autobiography, but without all the detail. It is a personal reflection on how things have turned out thus far in our lives. It is also to consider how much of our progress to this point has been due to us steering our own boat, and how much has been due to simply drifting with the current. And conversely to pick up on the skills that we might have gained and will be able to use in the future. With this in mind, we can also have a look at where any of the concepts covered in this book have been used, or where using something from this book could have been useful.

Ask yourself questions as you conduct the audit. Was I just drifting at this point? Was I making positive choices and changes? Were there good things that happened and helped me? Were there negative things that happened and have set me back, or even put me off ever trying again? Did I make this choice as I assumed that the alternative were thing I CANNOT do? Am I looking at something that is valuable to me and should be put on my values list?

Very importantly, in doing this, it is not an opportunity to beat yourself up over wrong decisions or weep over lost opportunities. Rather, it is a chance to take a fairly neutral view on your life-path thus far and consider what sort of difference taking some of the suggestions in this book might have made. We can then judge which bits of this book might be useful in the future and which less so. OK, let us carry on. It is up to you where you start. You might move backwards and forwards in time a bit. You might start with a general shape or summary of your life and then start to fill in the details. You can start earlier or later. You can even start at the end and work backwards, or in the middle and work outwards. Importantly, even though you will be asking yourself questions about what got you to where you are now in a fairly neutral way – this can still be difficult stuff to deal with emotionally. Make sure that you have some private and uninterrupted time to yourself. And pre-arrange some treat for yourself at the end of however long a session you set aside. Give yourself a reward, a film with a hot chocolate, taking the dog for a walk, or a bubble bath/Jacuzzi etc. I found it useful to 'pretend' I was writing and explain things for someone else to read (and as it turns out that is the case as you are actually reading this). Originally I wrote it straight through and then revisited it several times and noted where there might be things to learn (positive and negative) from the concepts in this book.

My Life Audit

So how did I get to where I am now? Well I nearly didn't. Most of my working career has been spent in Information Technology (IT). I sort of fell into IT after university when I graduated back in 1984. Almost prehistoric times compared with the technology that is available now. I didn't even apply for my first two or three jobs. I managed to get some experience of programming FORTRAN (Don't ask! – very old computer language, although it did get man to the moon – although not my code) on mainframes. That was enough to get into one of the largest IT companies in the world and train first as a Systems Engineer and then as a Sales Consultant. A decent career, with a decent salary and decent prospects. Highlights included taking clients on a private jet to the South of France and 'exotic' business trips all round Europe as well as the USA (East Coast Only) and South America. However, using one of the Aphorisms;

"If you don't know where you are going, that is exactly where you will end up".

And that is exactly where I did end up; Somewhere I hadn't chosen and a life that was becoming more and more incongruent. Of course, I didn't realise this at the time, but it is interesting that I have immediately homed in and started my audit at the point when I really realised that what I was doing did not add up to the life I wanted to lead. Something needed to change. [Maybe this is where you are right now.]

After following a random path dictated more by luck than judgement I ended up somewhere I didn't recognise. I wasn't interested in what I was doing, didn't get any satisfaction from it, and felt that I was just treading water to pay the bills. It didn't help that I was sometimes working 80 hour weeks out of some strange and possibly misguided sense of... well, sense of what? Maybe a belief that this was what was necessary 'now' in order to enjoy the results of my toil 'later'. [Does that ring any bells with anyone?] I was not leading a congruent life and my journey and destination were about as far adrift from each other as it was possible to get. I was in pre-contemplation mode at this point in my life. I was not particularly unhappy, but I had certainly not considered that there might be alternatives. I had not asked myself the question;

"Imagine you only had one life, what would you do with it?"

But thinking about this, there must have been a time when I had an idea of where I did want to get to and what I wanted to do. If you had asked me as a child of about 14 or 15 years old what I wanted to do, I would have said that I wanted to sail around the world. At this time only a handful of people had actually done this. As life moved on I gradually pushed this idea into the future; kicking the can down the street as they say. I did revisit it a few times, did some sailing courses and got very close to buying a small boat on several occasions with a revised dream of maybe going out sailing at weekends as long as it fitted in with work. I subscribed to all the sailing magazines for years and became quite an armchair expert.

But sailing around the world is not really a job. So what about a job; what would I have said I wanted to do 'when I grew up'. Well I enjoyed fixing cars and was quite good at it. So maybe a mechanic? That would work. However, I finished school (with very few qualifications by the way) and got a job as a laboratory technician (That is where I learned to program in FORTRAN). It could have just as easily been as a car mechanic. So I drifted into that. The good thing about this job was that I was required to go to college one day per week and take some technical qualifications that were at the right level so that I could apply for university if I wanted. My thinking was that I could do a technical degree of some sort. Again, just drifting towards something. Then something quite key happened. I found a book at home ('Language, Truth and Logic' by A.J Ayer) and picked it up. It was a very dense philosophy book about something called Logical Positivism. I had never heard of Logical Positivism and quite honestly did not understand a word of it, but I kept on reading until the end. I still didn't understand a word of it. It was a 'proper' philosophy book written for philosophers. I started to wonder what it would be like to actually be able to understand a book like that. After all, if others could understand it, then surely so could I – couldn't I? [Remember that this is one of the tests to see if something should be on the CANNOT list or not]. So, for almost the first time I decided to steer myself in a direction I wanted to go. I did some reading around philosophy and started to look at university courses. I eventually decided on one that also combined psychology and sociology with philosophy and got a place. It is worth saying at this point that no-one else in my immediate family had gone to university. In fact I didn't know anyone who had. I really didn't know what to expect. This was a real moment of serendipity. Looking back I can't remember how I managed to take such a 'risky' step into the unknown.

In brief, I loved it. [The important thing in the context of this book, is that I had said 'STOP' – let me have a think about what I actually want to do, what do I need to do it, and am I willing to put the effort in. For the first time I had effectively followed the sort of steps I have been advocating in the previous pages, and more importantly, it had paid off.] By a completely unforeseen coincidence Sir A.J. Ayer (who had written the book that inspired me) was a visiting professor at my chosen university and I got the opportunity to write and present a paper to him during my first year. – I found out later that all the postgraduates and many of the second and third years had been asked and they all said "no". Too nervous to present to this 'famous' philosopher. In my naivety I jumped at the chance and actually enjoyed the experience of having every single one of my arguments metaphorically torn limb from limb.

Logical Positivism wasn't really for me, but I became fascinated by some of the continental philosophers; in particular the German ones. So again, in the spirit of figuring out what I really wanted out of life and being prepared to do some work to get there, I went to night school to learn German and applied to study philosophy for a semester at Hamburg University in the North of Germany. I just scraped in as a Gästhorer (literally a guest listener) and left every lecture with a headache through concentrating so hard.

So looking back, this should really be the point at which I discover that I am allowed to decide for myself what I want to do and have the confidence that I can put a plan in place and actually achieve it. Maybe sail round the world after all? I did develop another plan whilst at university. I decided that I would take my sailboat (imaginary sailboat) up to the Scottish Islands and sit and write philosophy books. However, that really came to nothing as I considered that there is not a lot of money in writing about philosophy, and besides, my finals were looming and I probably needed to get a 'proper' job. I lost focus and started to drift again. Being at university had been a positive phase. Unfortunately I viewed it as just that; a phase. It didn't occur to me that what had made it such a positive experience was that I had been living congruently – what I should have done at this point is to

160

seek something out (work or career) that would also be congruent. [I am not beating myself up by saying that 'I should have done' something different. It is simply what happened.]

I moved to London with a couple of university friends and started to apply for jobs – any job that paid would do. I applied for, and got offered a job in banking and another in publishing. I think you can see what a random spread that is even from just two examples. However, a friend had passed my details on to an employment consultant (does that job still exist?) and because of my brief spell of computer programming prior to university I was offered, and took, a job in computing based simply on a slightly higher salary. The same consultant, rather unprofessionally, contacted me about a year later and found me a new job out of London with a major IT company at what seemed to me at the time a dizzy five figure salary of £10,000 (below what we would now consider to be the minimum liveable wage). So I moved out of London and spend the next twenty years moving through various positions in computing with various companies. I also got married, bought a house, moved house, had children and went through the typical gamut of some very good times and some very difficult times. Nevertheless I had, again, ended up in a place that I really didn't recognised, and couldn't quite see how I had got there. Again, I was back in the realm of;

"If you don't know where you are going, that is exactly where you will end up".

I had managed to get to this 'place' twice in a row. I didn't really know where I was, and I didn't really know where to go next. I had no idea of what to do except work towards retirement and maybe buy a boat if I was still

161

physically fit enough. I was very unfit at that point from working long hours, but had managed to kick the smoking habit as I decided that whatever else happened I was not going to be a smoking parent. I also had a massive mortgage on the house and the IT level salary needed to sustain it which was more than I could earn elsewhere. I felt stuck. But I did manage to include some of the typical mid-life crisis toys into the mix including both a Ducati and Harley Davidson motorcycle – although not at the same time.

As I mentioned right at the beginning of the introduction, sometimes it is life events that precipitate a change, or start a thought rolling. My oldest child has quite a profound learning disability and has had very demanding additional needs from an early age. As parents, we did our best, got worn out, and tried not to become too isolated from the rest of the world. It can be quite lonely dealing with something that the rest of the people you know really have no experience of. Then one evening we were invited to a talk being given from someone who worked with children with similar difficulties. A couple of peripatetic support workers had noticed that a lot of parents were having the same experience of feeling isolated, lost and powerless. So they put the event together and invited people. It was quite strange going straight from being 'the only parents in the world' going through this to sitting in a room with forty other people in a very similar situation.

This turned out to be another key point in my life. A few parents including myself decided that this could not be allowed to be just a one-off event. We formed a committee and started to organise. I volunteered to become the Chairman and was voted in. We kept regular monthly talks from experts going as well as arranging social events for the children and lobbying local authorities (including schools etc) to improve facilities and support for both children and their families. This became quite time consuming and demanding. It was also, of course, unpaid. I soon started to realise that I was enjoying this work a lot more than my day-job in IT. It was much more rewarding and satisfactory, and importantly, much more aligned with my values – the things that were truly important to me. This aspect of my life became very congruent, even if my 9 to 5 salaried job wasn't. I had accidently discovered what it was like to be congruent again.

I considered a career change at this point, but felt that it would be impossible as even the best paid jobs within the caring professions were paid at a level much lower than I was working in IT, and wouldn't pay the mortgage. The important thing here is that I had fallen into the trap of slamming shut a door in front of me without even considering how I might be able to make it work. I put it firmly on my CANNOT list of things. Think about it. How strange is that that I could see an alternative preferred future that would be more aligned with my true values, but I stuck with what I was doing (which by this time it is fair to say I actually hated) even though my past experience (going to university etc) had proved to me that pretty much everything was possible. Why? Too risky? Fear of the unknown? Anxiety? [possibly lots of Negative Automatic Thoughts which I will cover in the next section]. Better the devil you know? Procrastination? All of these and more. I am not beating myself up and blaming myself for not realising this earlier, I am just curious. I was mistakenly believing at this point that although I now had a much better idea of where I wanted to go, I didn't think I could get there from where I was. Looking back on it I realise that I had simply believed my CANNOT list and not challenged it.

Moving on a few years, I did try and escape, but not in the right direction. The IT industry became very risky from a job security point of view and I decided that at the very least I should take some control back by becoming my own boss. This can be a very positive thing. [And is the thing that many of you might be thinking of.] To mitigate the perceived risk a bit I decided to go for a franchise (By franchise I mean here a proven business model where you effectively licence the business method from the person who set up the first one). However, unfortunately I chose a franchise that turned out to be crooked. Many people were taken in. We very nearly managed to turn things around and got very close to salvaging things. But the end result was that we lost all our savings and had to sell the house to pay off debts. I was left with just enough to buy a cheap car and put down a few months rental on a small house – which was actually delightful and in the middle of the countryside. Unfortunately the stress of the previous year or so turned out to be too much and, as often happens, this point was also the end of my marriage.

"Imagine you were starting with nothing. How would you get to where you want to go?"

This is not quite an Aphorism as such, but can be quite a useful tool when you are at the stage of figuring out what you want to do. I had blocked a lot of possibilities because I 'knew' what salary I needed in order to keep paying the mortgage. One option I had thought about was to study and get some new qualifications. But this seemed impossible as I simply couldn't afford it – or so I thought. [This had been on my CANNOT list for some time and I had never challenged it until this point]. However, what I found was that, bizarrely, when I was starting with nothing, it was possible. [I am not suggesting that you should give away everything in order to start something new. But at least in the stage of figuring out what your preferred future might be, you can imagine how you would achieve it if you were starting with nothing. Sometimes that is easier to work out than starting from where you are. A bit like our lost traveller trying to get to Plumpton right at the beginning of the book.]

Well, I didn't actually have to imagine I was starting with nothing. This was exactly the position I found myself in – I had an unreliable second hand car and the very kind loan of a static caravan (trailer) to stay in. This takes us to just over ten years ago (again writing this in 2018), and really was the critical point when the penny finally dropped that I did only have one life and it was up to me to decide what I wanted to do with it. "If I don't make it happen, no-one else will". I needed to grab the tiller and steer the boat – and that is what happened. It was also the point when that most useful Aphorism kicked in and I was able to assemble the previous elements of my experience and make a plan that I could now follow.

"Imagine you only had one life, what would you do with it?"

That is the end of the actual Life Audit example.

So that is really the point at which I would stop my own Life Audit if I were looking back from the point where I wanted to start to follow the suggestions in this book. But if I were you, I would want to know if the author of this book had actually walked the talk and followed the 'advice' he has been giving out. Did I practice what I have been preaching? Well, not all of the ideas I have laid out in this book were fully developed at that point. However, yes I have followed and still do follow the ideas I have laid out. So, I will continue in summary form just so that you can see what happened next.

I literally started drawing things out on sheets of paper to see what my preferred future was and how I could get there. I made little cartoons of metaphors. I had stick figures walking across tightropes (I seem to remember that one of the tightropes was over a lake full of sharks) and climbing mountains, all in glorious technicolour. I went through a lot of the congruency tests covered in the first part of this book. I also decided that this would not be a one off 'all in' exercise, but I would remain on guard (unlike my university days) in case I drifted again. I drew up a congruency list – although I didn't realise that this was what I was doing at this stage.

- From experience I knew that study or retraining would not be allowed to be an obstacle. In fact it is part of being congruent for me that I am always wanting to learn new things.
- I wanted to work with people. And very specifically, not computers.
- I wanted to help people who through no fault of their own were disadvantaged through lack of life-chances.
- I wanted to help to stand up for people who didn't have their own voice. That is, to advocate for and with them.
- I wanted to improve my work/life balance and not get too focused on 'just work' as I had done before.

These were some of the things that were important to me and gave value and meaning to my life.

At the time I did not know about congruency as I have described it in this book or even the Miracle Question, or many of the techniques I covered in the first section right at the start of this book on figuring out what I wanted to do. However, I had done a lot of project management in my business career and felt comfortable that once I knew what I wanted to do I would be able to get there.

I tested out a few hypothetical preferred futures by looking at as many different careers, jobs, college courses and university courses as possible and examined how closely they fitted my wants and values. Options included:

- Barrister
- Social Worker
- Counsellor
- Therapist
- Teacher
- And a few more

I did quite a detailed analysis of each option. I drew up a table on a sheet of paper and wrote each of these down the side. Along the top I wrote a few headings including, how long to qualify, cost of study, grants access, employability prospects, etc. I then put ticks or crosses along with comments under each heading for each option.

There was a shortage of both Social Workers and Teachers at the time. In short, I managed to get onto a Social Work course and qualified two years afterwards. I then worked with children in care for two years. Following this I took a volunteer post in Romania working in a Mental Health Hospital with residential patients. This involved spending all the money I had saved and starting from zero again. But because it was done with the knowledge that I was being 10/10 congruent, this did not worry me and it was probably the best 'job' I have ever had. I then went back to university whilst working which is where I qualified in CBT. Although I have changed jobs a number of times since deciding to live a more congruent life, all of them have been deliberate changes through me steering my own origami boat in the direction I wanted to go – and I have enjoyed all of them. I am now getting to a point where I would like to retire from full-time work, but continue on a congruent path (or river). One thing I really wanted to do was to put all the ideas I had developed and gathered and put them into book form. This is what I am doing right now – typing the very book that you are reading. I hope that the ideas in it are as useful for you as they have been for me.

So what's next? What about that dream of sitting in a boat on a Scottish Loch and writing Philosophy books? Well maybe that's next, and maybe I have started that journey already. But I am a little bit older now and Scotland can be cold. So maybe the Mediterranean Sea might be a warmer prospect…

Making Sense of Anxiety

So why have a section on Anxiety in this book. Well, Anxiety in its various guises is one of the most powerful emotions you have. In particular it is the emotion that will try and stop you doing things or making any changes in your life. And as it stops you doing things it becomes stronger. Anxiety both creates avoidance and feeds on avoidance. Once it has a grip on stopping you doing something it will become bigger and more difficult to deal with. Anxiety can stop you from making the changes you need to get to the life you want. Worse, it can even stop you at the earlier stage of even imagining what your preferred future might look like.

Because of this I felt it was important to include something on Anxiety as it is a very powerful factor in many people's lives and it can quite literally stop us in our tracks. And can certainly stop us moving towards our preferred future. One of the basic and big problems with Anxiety is that it feeds itself. By that I mean that if we do nothing about it, it gets stronger and can dominate our life more as time goes on. Briefly, Anxiety can make us avoid things and change our behaviour, and avoiding things feeds Anxiety and makes us avoid things even more. There are many different forms of Anxiety, and everybody's experience of it is unique to them. My aim in this short section is to try and explain what Anxiety is, how it works, and to open up a pathway that could help to manage and overcome it. It is not going to be a full Self-Help Anxiety guide. However, I hope that after you have read this section you will be in a better position to understand what to do next; whether that is to engage with a professional therapist, or go for a self-guided approach. I also want to give you hope. Anxiety is natural and normal and can be managed. Unfortunately for those suffering from Anxiety, it seems completely unnatural, weird, debilitating and permanent.

I have worked with people whose lives have been blighted by anxiety for several years. I mainly use CBT (Cognitive Behavioural Therapy) but also SFBT (Solution-Focused Brief Therapy) techniques. Anxiety is awful. If you suffer from it or know people who have it, you already realise this. It can make you avoid situations and really restrict what you are able to do. In the worst cases, people can't even leave the house any more. I have capitalised Anxiety up to here simply to highlight it as an actual thing worthy of proper noun status, but to make the reading easier I will put it back in lower case (anxiety) just to make the reading easier on the eye. But that doesn't reduce its status.

I want to really try and get under the skin of what anxiety is and try and explain that it is actually based on normal and useful reactions and processes, but these have simply spiralled completely out of control and become anything but normal and useful. I also want to explain how it can be brought back under control.

Consider this analogy. I am a really bad swimmer (this is true); I didn't learn to swim until I was a teenager. I used to think that maybe there were simply people who couldn't swim, and I was one of them. Every time I got in the water as a child I sort of sank, then flailed about a bit, and then coughed and spluttered as I swallowed and breathed in water. I tried the approach of reading books about swimming. Useful in their own right, they sort of explained all the general principles, but were not really sufficient for me to be able to claim that, "great, I can now swim". I had to do two things; firstly get in the water, and secondly practice – proper practice starting with first principles, not just flailing and hoping. Not pleasant at first, I found the water to be a really unnatural environment for me, and I really wanted to give up. But it was worth it in the end; I can now swim. Not brilliantly, but it is still swimming. The principle with anxiety is similar – we need to understand the principles and then get into the 'water' and practice. Sounds a bit strange so far doesn't it. What do you mean, 'practice with anxiety'? It will become clearer. Carry on reading.

In my experience I believe it is absolutely vital to first try and get an understanding of what anxiety is and what is going on in our brains and bodies. However, I don't mean that we need to have an understanding of the neurophysiological (if that is even a word) things going on in our head. I believe that the understanding we need is like that of a 'compelling argument'. By compelling I mean that once we understand it, we then believe it enough to follow what it says. I find that once the penny drops and people really get what is going on, they are much more willing to 'get in the (metaphorical) water' and start treatment. So my task here is to try and explain what is going on with anxiety in a clear and compelling way.

I like to use a lot of metaphors and examples to describe this. We have powerful imaginations and can conjure powerful images. In fact, often it is this imagination that fuels our anxiety as we imagine the worse possible consequences and totally believe that this is what will happen. Sometimes the metaphors I use can be quite light hearted, but that doesn't mean that I don't take the subject seriously. I take it completely seriously. I have also found that dealing with the problem of anxiety can seem quite counter intuitive. By this I mean that if we simply try and sort it out by battling against it, it can get worse. A bit like falling into quicksand and flailing around and fighting to get out. This just makes us sink quicker. The trick with quicksand is to stay cool, flatten ourselves out and make gentle movements to escape; very counter intuitive. Anxiety is very similar; if we fight it anxiety will fight back. True, I have met a number of people who have figured out how to deal with their own anxiety very successfully. But for the majority of us, some external help is needed. Talking of external help, if anxiety is a significant problem for you, I really advise that you do go to your doctor and ask to be pointed towards someone who can help. I would also advise that you get help from someone who works in an evidence based way. This means a therapist who is working with a proven therapeutic approach such as CBT. Support for anxiety conditions is getting better and many health systems worldwide are realising that the cost of not dealing with anxiety problems is greater than the cost of doing something about it. Nevertheless I do understand how difficult it can be to make that first step and ask for help. If all this short section does is to give you confidence that there is help available, and you go out and seek it, then I will be very happy indeed.

I am not claiming to provide a detailed explanation of the process and mechanisms of anxiety in intricate detail. There are books out there that will give you a synapse by synapse explanation of exactly what is going on. My aim here is to simplify as much as possible in order to make the explanation useful. That also means explaining things in a way which means we can put these ideas to use in the actual real lived world. However, that does not mean dumbing things down. As (I believe) Einstein said, we should always explain things as simply as possible, but no simpler.

I don't claim that anything in this section is original. In fact it would be worrying if it was as I am attempting to put things forward with a proven evidential track record. Unfortunately I can't remember where all of the ideas will have come from, but I am very grateful to colleagues, esteemed experts who I have met, been taught by, and read their books. I am most grateful to the people I have worked with to help them with their Anxiety problems who have helped me to turn my theoretical knowledge into practical experience.

Anxiety is normal

No it's not. It's not normal, it's horrible. It's ruining my life, you say. There must be something wrong with me. I can't face things that others take in their stride. Also, it is bizarre that I am happy to do dangerous things like bungee jump but I can't even get on a bus without having a panic attack. That cannot be normal, surely? Actually, it is normal. By 'normal' I mean that the processes our brain and body are going through are normal processes. Unfortunately they have become miss-calibrated (or too sensitive) in certain areas and have become decidedly 'unhelpful'. Unhelpful is quite a small word to describe just how debilitating these normal, but unhelpful, processes have become.

We would be in deep trouble if we never had anxious moments. We wouldn't be able to react to a genuinely dangerous situation. However, if our lives are dominated by anxiety all the time then that equals misery. Even if not all the time, it can limit our lives if anxiety starts to rule and stops us doing things; like meeting people, going out, applying for a new job or trying new things. Also, anxiety can be a miserable and debilitating experience; it just feels physically and mentally awful.

But anxiety is the result of very normal, and useful, processes. That doesn't sound right does it? Let's have a closer look at what is going on.

So what is anxiety for?

Well, basically, it is a normal and useful self-protection mechanism that can sometimes go wrong and then become stuck in the 'wrong mode'.

Imagine 40,000 years ago we were sitting in our cave with dangerous animals wandering around outside. We were hunter gatherers then. Life was tough and we had to have our wits about us. Every now and then we would suddenly encounter a life threatening dangerous situation and we would need to act quickly and muster almost superhuman abilities to either flee (the preferred option) or fight our way out of trouble. The part of our brain that deals with this became excellent at what it does. It reacts quicker than any other part of the brain and is basically the trump card – it pretty much always wins any argument about what to do. In fact there is no debate in our heads about what to do; we just go into automatic mode. This part of the brain is about the size of a baked bean and is called the Amygdala. It is brilliantly effective and hasn't really changed much in 40,000 years. So, before we look at what happens when it goes wrong, let's explore what it does and why it does it a bit more first.

Let us step forward in time out of our cave and back into the 21st century. Here is an analogy to follow. Let us imagine that we are in a modern office room. Most modern offices have a decent fire alarm system. We can also have a smoke alarm, plus heat detection, and movement detection devices. I have even worked in rooms that monitor the Carbon Dioxide levels. Each of these detectors are linked to a central alarm system. When the level of whatever it is the detector is detecting reaches a certain level, the alarm is triggered. Usually this means a ringing bell, siren and/or flashing lights. Everyone in the office stops what they are doing and follows a protocol; the fire drill. – Leaving by certain routes etc, and only returning when we are told it is safe. We don't question whether there is a real fire or not – it is far safer to simply follow the procedures. But, as most of us know, the alarm can sometimes be a 'false' one. For example, I worked in a building where the heat detector in the boiler room was set too low. It was going off at heat levels that were far from exceptional or dangerous and the boiler room naturally became hotter than the other rooms. However, the alarm went off and the building was evacuated each time. Better safe than sorry. Eventually an engineer adjusted the sensitivity level and we had no more false alarms.

Our Amygdala is a bit like a fire alarm system. It is linked to many of our body's detectors (more details soon) and also triggers the 'evacuation fire drill procedure'. It doesn't make that many decisions, it simply goes off and reacts to what it has detected. Unhelpful and problematic anxiety reactions are a bit like the situation above regarding the miscalibrated boiler room detector where the anxiety alarm is being set off too often and is no longer helpful as what it is reacting to is not an actual life or death situation, but our Amygdala is reacting as if it were. Now, wouldn't it be nice if we could get a 'brain engineer' to just turn down our Amygdala and adjust it to the right level. No more false alarm. The bad news is that it isn't quite that simple. We can't just turn it down. Even worse news, we can't just avoid what makes us anxious and wait for it to go away. In fact, avoidance is very thing that feeds anxiety the most. Oh dear, this desire to be able to manage our anxiety levels does not seem to be going well does it. How can we overcome this 40,000 year old part of the brain that is much quicker and dominates the more rational part?

There is good news. The good news is that rather than adjust it, we can train it. That sounds weird, doesn't it? Train our brains? What on earth does that mean? Well, I will need to go into this a bit further before that will make sense – but it will. It is similar to the earlier idea of learning to swim by practicing from first principles. Just like with swimming where we initially need to get into safe calm (and hopefully warm) water and practice swimming. With anxiety we will need to start to practice with safe, but slightly anxiety provoking, situations and allow our Amygdala to gradually accept that it isn't actually a life or death situation.

Right, let's jump back into our cave 40,000 years ago and wander outside to get some berries. Our Amygdala will be on super high alert mode. It will be more than just vigilant; it will be hypervigilant. After all the stakes are high. If some great big clawed, long toothed beast sneaks up on us we won't even have a chance to use our famous Fight or Flight reaction. We'll be done for - eaten. No, The Amygdala wants to pick up the smallest signs and then

176

react very quickly. So, we hear an ominous sound in the bushes. Footsteps (paw steps!) coming our way. The Amygdala kicks in and before we even have a chance to think or assess the situation it sets off a whole multitude of physical processes in our body. There is adrenalin produced (to give us an immediate power boost) which starts pulsing through our body, our heart rate increases to send oxygenated blood to where it is needed. In fact, blood is taken away from our unessential activities (like digesting food) and sent to the bigger leg and arm muscles (used for fighting or running away). Sweat starts pouring out to cool us down ready for what is to come.

And then we take to flight, we run. And by the way, I don't need to be able to run faster than a sabre-toothed tiger, I just need to be able to run faster than you in order to survive; think about it. Or we Fight; quite literally for our lives. In either case our body has moved from being a sedate wood trimmed station wagon estate car to a thoroughbred Italian sports car (I said I would mix metaphors – I know they didn't have such vehicles 40,000 years ago). A third possibility is that we Freeze. This might be safer if the creature hasn't seen us. We don't want to break cover and attract attention. If the danger passes we feel wretched as our body is shaking from the adrenalin that is not being used and the queasy sick feeling from our stomach that has stopped working. We are cold and dripping with sweat. But we have survived and we are safe. We can also see at this point how it is most probably the humans with the fastest and most hypervigilant Amygdales that survived and the ones with sloppy Amygdales that perished. Hence we, you and me, are the result of ancestors with very hypervigilant Amygdales. So we survived. Unfortunately in the last 40,000 years our

Amygdala hasn't really changed much, but the world we live in has.

Anxiety is only a problem if it becomes unhelpful. And unhelpful is not a big enough word to describe how unhelpful it can be. Let's get back into our time machine and jump forward 40,000 years back to the present day. There are no sabre-tooth tigers. However, our Amygdala and associated mechanisms have not changed at all. These mechanisms can still be useful. If we are jogging slowly past a gate and a big dog jumps out barking loudly, all our systems kick in and we high-tail it up the road at a superhuman rate. But in the main, for most of us, 21st century western life is not as hazardous as that we faced back in the stone ages. So here is the thing. If your Amygdala does kick in, even if the perceived threat is not real, our physical and emotional reaction is exactly the same as it would be if we were facing a life or death situation. The threat might not be real, but our reaction certainly is.

How we risk assess situations

You might think that you don't risk assess situations in everyday life. Surely that is an actual job that someone qualified does in order to make sure that things are safe to use. Buildings, walkways, bridges, factory equipment, toys etc. Unfortunately, our Amygdala can get out of hand and do risk assessments for us without engaging the more rational and thinking part of our brain at all. The Amygdala simply goes for the worst case scenario every time. And the decision to avoid something is made before we even realise that the risk assessment has happened. The key here is to understand what our Amygdala is doing and then start to get in the habit of doing a more reasonable assessment of the situation based on facts and reality, and gradually train our Amygdala that not everything difficult is actually a life or death situation.

If you were about to build a large Chemical factory next to a highly populated town you would almost certainly be expected to do some sort of risk assessment. There would probably be some sort of local outcry (quite understandably) if you didn't. Also, you would be expected to put in plenty of safety measures to ensure that the likelihood of an accident happening was very small – and if there was an accident, measures to make sure it would have a minimum impact and those living around the factory could be 'rescued' or saved in some way.

There are, of course, plenty of examples from all around the world where things have gone wrong, badly wrong, and the outcomes have not gone well. Hopefully we learn from such things and feed them into our next risk assessment.

One formal way of doing a risk assessment is known as FMEA (Failure Mode and Effect Analysis). A very superficial overview of this is:

Failure Mode – What type of things can go wrong and how likely are they to go wrong?

Failure Effect – If they do go wrong what is the overall severity?

We can also add to these two factors and consider what to do if it does all go horribly pear shaped. We can consider what the person (or people) in immediate control can do to help and Recover the situation (stop it getting worse), and what others outside people can do to Rescue those affected and get them out of harm's way.

For example, there might only be a 0.001% chance of the factory blowing up (Failure Mode). But if it did then the whole town would be wiped out (Failure Effect). Also, once a chain of events had been set in place there would be no stopping it and getting things back to normal (Recovery) – so no way out of this Failure. To make things worse the nearest rescue services are miles away over a mountain and across a deep sea (Rescue). So even though the chances of the accident happening are very small indeed, the consequences are catastrophic. We would probably decide not to build the factory.

We actually do risk assessments like this in everyday life all the time without even realising it. Let us take a trivial example, I go into an exam and I drop my pencil. I know (from experience) that there is a high probability that the lead inside will have (at best) broken or (at worst) shattered. The chance of it shattering might be 90% (Mode). The consequences (Effect) are trivial and I can mitigate them; sharpen it a few times or throw it away and use one of the many spares I have at hand (Recovery). Also I can always borrow a pencil from a friend (Rescue). So I don't give this an overall high mark and am happy to carry my pencil into the exam. In this instance the stakes are so low that even our hypervigilant Amygdala will probably take some time off and not become involved. Although I have known people who will take large pencil cases stuffed with spare pencils and pens and be in a constant state of semi-panic that none of them will work and the exam will be a total disaster.

Unfortunately, when we have problems with anxiety the Amygdala takes over and assesses all of these variables before our rational brain has a chance of a look-in. It simply puts everything at either the maximum or the minimum in order to make us avoid the situation as much as possible. Our Amygdala rates the 'catastrophe' as being 100% likely to happen, and it will be 100% devastating when it does

180

happen. Added to this I won't be able to recover at all (I have no skills or capabilities or presence of mind) and no-one will help me – I will be alone.

One of the most feared of all things we do in life is speaking in public. In front of class, giving a speech at a wedding, or a presentation at work, college or school etc. So, if Public Speaking is high up on our most feared anxiety list of things then we would normally avoid it. Let us look at an example of how a risk assessment ruled by our Amygdala might work for this speaking in public scenario:

Failure Mode: I am going to mess up big time. It will be a disaster. I will stumble over my words, shake uncontrollably, turn red, I will get my facts wrong, I will forget what I was going to say, or not be able to read what I have written, or I might just freeze and do nothing just staring blankly out at the audience. I put a 99-100 % probability on this happening. These are all examples of Negative Automatic Thoughts (NATs). We believe NATs as if they were facts even though they are not based on any evidence.

Effect: People will judge me, they will think I am an idiot, they will laugh at me, I will be openly mocked afterwards, I will never be able to face them again. I will probably faint or be sick on stage. I also rate this at 99% or higher! Even more NATs.

Recovery: There is nothing I can do to stop these awful things from happening – apart from running out of the room before I have to actually do it. I have no skills as a public speaker. As soon as I stand up the spiral into disaster will have started and I am doomed to failure and ridicule. My chances of recovering the situation and getting through it are 0% - 1% at the absolute most.

Rescue: No-one will help me. They all want me to fail, they are willing me to fail. It will be fun for them to see me make an absolute fool of myself. The chance that anyone will help or support me if (when!!) things go wrong is 0%. I am not even going to think it might be as high as 1% in this instance.

Does that ring any bells? Now in actual fact, although some of the things listed are possible, our belief percentages are way out of line. Our Amygdala is exaggerating the 'danger' deliberately to try and make us avoid the situation. Thinking back on how this worked 40,000 years ago; if I 100% believed that there was a tiger outside that was going to eat me, and that I could not fight it or run away, and that no one was going to come to my aid. Then there is no way that I am going to go outside and find out. And if I don't find out, then I never find out if there was a tiger or not. But as far as my protective Amygdala is concerned, I don't get eaten, and that is all it cares about. Better safe than sorry.

One way to start to allow the more rational part of our brain to have a say in doing the risk assessments is to start practicing doing them calmly with the more rational part of our brain. If we don't, the Amygdala will simply take over. So for example, try taking a recent example of an anxiety provoking situation from your own experience. Write down the risk percentages as you believed them at the time, based on the Negative Automatic Thoughts (NATs) that came into your head from your Amygdala. Write down the NATs as well if you can remember them. The numbers might come out similar to the 'speaking in public' example we covered just now:

Failure Mode – "I am going to mess up big time" – 99% believed

Effect – "people will judge me" – 99% believed

Recovery – "there is nothing I can do to prevent disaster" – 1% chance of recovering the situation

Rescue – "No one will help me, they want me to fail" – 1% chance of rescue

Now do the same, but this time based on a calm and objective look at the facts. You will most probably find that the percentages change somewhat. For example, using the same scenario;

Failure Mode – "Actually, I don't like public speaking and I might make a few mistakes, but I will get through it" – Revise previous probability percentage of total disaster down to 30%.

Effect – "In fact people will not openly mock me even if I did make a mistake, I have never seen this happen in any presentation situation" – Revise previous probability percentage down to 20%

Recovery – "I do know my subject, and if I breath and speak slowly, I can get through it until the end even if I do stumble a bit" – maybe I do have some skills I will revise the probability of being able to recover to about 50%.

Rescue – "We are all in the same boat, the people I am speaking in front of want me to do well, they are interested in what I am saying. If it goes wrong my tutor (manager, friend) can step in and help out". There is a possibility that others will help, I will change this to 45%.

Notice that the percentages will probably not change from 100% right down to 0% for Failure and Effect Mode (or 0% to 100% for Recovery and Rescue respectively). There is a chance that things will go wrong. Even great and accomplished presenters will make mistakes occasionally, or some visual aid will fail. However, realistically this does not happen very often, and if it does recovery is possible.

Try a few of these scenarios using things that happened in the past to get used to the process. Now have a practice – time to get in the water. Actually think of a mildly anxiety provoking situation you could try. Write out your worst case risk assessment as you believe it right now. Also write out the Negative Automatic Thoughts (NATs) that pop into your head. But alongside the NATs write down a more positive potential outcome so that you will have something to compare against. Now go and try it out. Actually go through the situation, don't avoid it. Rather than focusing purely on the anxiety and how horrible it feels, observe what is going on around you against the earlier risk assessment you made. Also keep a mental note of your actual anxiety level throughout this practice (0 being no anxiety, and 10 being maximum anxiety). Review your observations afterwards and write them down. See if there is anything you have learned from your practice. Try the same thing again several times and see if there is any improvement. See if your anxiety rating starts to go down. Hopefully you will be able to start to challenge yourself more and try out situations that are higher up the anxiety scale. What you are doing is training your Amygdala that these situations are not actually life or death and there is no need to set all the alarms off.

So let's talk about Avoidance a bit more as it is so important.

I said earlier that avoidance feeds anxiety like nothing else. Again, 40,000 years ago this made sense. It was much more sensible to avoid needing to Fight or Flight as much as possible. Better safe than sorry, as we said before. Both of these things take up a lot of energy. Energy basically comes from metabolising food. And food is scarce, difficult to get – and with sabre-toothed tigers out there, dangerous as well. So, back in those days we are not going to wander out for a lovely bracing walk. We stayed in our cave based on our well justified, belief that there were dangerous things out there that wanted to eat us.

Avoidance nowadays is also based on belief. It is problematic and unhelpful when that belief is patently not based on fact. How we build those believes is a complicated matter. Sometimes it takes one small event. Sometimes many. Sometimes we cannot remember how it might have come about. For example an abnormal phobia of dogs (as opposed to a normal respect for those dogs I don't know) might have started with a bad experience as a child, or as an adult. Our belief systems are complex and the root of them is, for the most part, hidden. They can also be the source of many of the things on our CANNOT list.

Let us use a slight strange example. Let us imagine that you and I are working in a small office with a corridor outside leading to the reception area and the front entrance. For some reason I have a real heightened phobia of tigers. I can't go to the zoo and I really don't even like watching them on TV documentaries. This is normally not a problem as in the small town where I work there is no chance whatsoever of encountering a tiger. However, let us imagine that for some reason I totally believe that there is a tiger sitting outside the office in the corridor. I believe it at least 95%. This may be irrational, but I believe it. The question is:

"How likely am I to go out into the corridor?"

I think it is fairly obvious that I am not going to go out into the corridor. No way!! I really believe there is a tiger out there – and I am terrified of them.

Now, let's forget the previous question. Try and get it out of your mind and I will ask another. Remember, I am sitting in the office with you. Consider this question:

"If I stay her in this office, will I get bitten by a tiger?"

No, of course I won't. There is no chance that I will be bitten by a tiger. It is actually quite a bizarre question. But with my heightened fear of tigers, I am very pleased to know that I will not get bitten by a tiger here in this office.

However, if we combine my belief that there is a tiger in the corridor and my knowledge that I will not get bitten by a tiger if I stay in the room, the anxiety controlled part of my brain comes to a conclusion. The conclusion is, "Staying here in this room is what is protecting me from being bitten by a tiger". Therefore I will stay in this room and avoid going out at all, ever; that will keep me safe. And we might ask; what is the problem with that? After all the aim is to not get bitten by a tiger and that is exactly what is happening; I am not going to get bitten by a tiger.

Well, a lot of us probably stay late in the office more often than we should. However, spending the rest of my life in my office is possibly not a good strategy. Also, by never going out I never find out that there is not a tiger in the corridor. I never find out that it is safe. I never find out that my belief is wrong. I keep my anxiety going. In this way we keep our beliefs going, which also keeps our risk assessment percentages completely skewed and unrealistic. And of course my conclusion that it is staying in the office that is saving me from being bitten by a tiger is completely wrong. The thing saving me from being bitten by a tiger is the fact that there are no tigers anywhere near – and never will be.

Let's look at a few more examples of how this might work.

There is a story of a man in London who walks around Piccadilly Circus with a bag of salt which he dips into and scatters on the ground. If you ask him why he is doing it he will say, "To keep the alligators away". If you retort that there are no alligators in Piccadilly Circus his reply would be, "that's because I am spreading the salt around". We can see the same non-logical connection here. He is spreading salt around – True. There are no alligators – True. However, our rational logic can tell us that there is absolutely no connection between someone spreading salt and alligators not appearing. But unfortunately human brains are very good at making connections even if they are false; making connections is an important part of how we make sense of the world. In his mind it is too dangerous to not spread the salt (better safe than sorry) – and after all, spreading salt is a small price to pay to keep London safe from alligators. (By the way if you are reading this in parts of Florida, please do not attempt to scare alligators out of your pool by sprinkling salt near them – it really does not work!)

A big trap is that we tend to believe that we should avoid doing something until our anxiety goes away. We think, "Once I get rid of my anxiety I will be able to go out and do the thing I can't do right now". I need to be able to give presentations, but I can't right now because of anxiety. Once the anxiety goes, I will be able to do presentations. Or, do evening classes to learn a new skill, start volunteering, join a gym, start driving lessons, talk to my boss about an idea I have etc. Unfortunately, it doesn't work like this. The way to defeat or manage anxiety is to practice experiencing it and start to learn (in effect training our Amygdala) that although the feeling of anxiety is unpleasant it will become less intense with more practice and exposure to the thing we fear. And as we practice, a bit like learning to swim, we become more confident in our ability to cope with situations. If we constantly avoid the situations that we fear then our anxiety will simply become worse and worse.

If you do decide to practice dealing with anxiety I would suggest that you start with something that is not right at the top of your anxiety scale. Make a list of the key things that are impacting on your life because of anxiety. Include things that you would normally avoid. If 10 is the most anxious and 0 is the least anxious then start with something you rank at around 3 or 4. After all, when I did finally get into the water and start to practice my swimming I didn't jump into a raging cold sea, I started in a warm shallow pool.

So in summary, the anxiety reaction is perfectly normal, but it can get out of control and become extremely unhelpful. Our Amygdala can behave like an overzealous guard dog that has slipped its collar and is running around barking trying to protect us from every piece of paper or leaf floating in the wind. It is no good shouting at the guard dog to stop; it will just sense more danger. We have to gently and persistently tell it that everything is alright and start to train it that not everything is dangerous and needs to be barked it. The other important thing about anxiety is that it rarely goes away on its own. The more we avoid things, the worse it gets. We have to train ourselves that we can actually tolerate some level of anxiety, and the more we practice this, the less the anxiety impacts us. We start to be able to manage it more and we start to avoid things and situations less. As we do this our world starts to open out for us and our confidence grows. As I said earlier, if anxiety is a significant problem for you, I would suggest that you seek help through your doctor and ask for an evidence based approach such as CBT. I hope this short section has at least given you some confidence that anxiety is something that can be treated and the negative impact of it reduced.

A note about procrastination.

Procrastination has been covered throughout the course of this book. Most of the techniques and Aphorisms have been designed to try and jolt us out of that horrible lethargy of procrastination. As stated right at the start, the whole focus of this book is to put forward techniques that are both useful and can be used. For example, the idea of using a planning diary where we use "today" as the basic planning unit is also designed to help to counter procrastination. I have seen many of the techniques we have covered used successfully to help people actually get out of their armchairs and start to make changes in their lives. But of course Procrastination is also a form of Avoidance. So might it be linked to anxiety in some way? There seems to be a possible link here towards putting things off with our anxiety driving us towards avoidance. Well there is some work that is starting to gain ground to say that the Amygdala might also play a role in Procrastination. The part of the brain that filters out distractions and keeps us on track in terms of fulfilling what we have set out to do is called the dorsal anterior cingulate cortex (dACC). The dACC also uses information from the Amygdala to decide what to do and what not to do. Put simply a more active Amygdala will tend to communicate more anxious messages to the dACC and cause the dACC to not do things, to put them off, to hesitate, to kick the can down the street, to procrastinate. This is possibly not surprising as we have already seen that the Amygdala tends to exaggerate when doing a risk assessment with the resulting outcome that we avoid doing things. It seems to me that the process with regards to procrastination is probably more subtle. We don't actually necessarily feel anxious about doing whatever it is that we need to do, the Amygdala just sends biased information to that part of our brain that ultimately makes the decision. From our perspective we don't necessarily feel anxious, we just keep putting stuff off until tomorrow. And as we have already covered, 'tomorrow' can be a very long time coming; if ever.

So the trick here is to consider whether or not your procrastination may be linked to the anxiety process and a false risk assessment, even if you do not feel particularly anxious about doing the activity or task you are procrastinating over. It is possible that the reason you are not feeling anxious is that you brain is tricking you into thinking that you will actually do the activity or task at some point – just not right now. The reason you don't feel anxious about it is that your Amygdala 'knows' that you will never actually get around to doing the task so why should you worry about it. So, what you need to do is to stop believing that you will do it tomorrow – that is a trick of the brain. What you need to do is remember and follow the aporism:

"It doesn't matter if you do it today or tomorrow. It matters if you do it today"

As I said at the start of this section, Anxiety is a big subject and I have not included a discussion on anxiety here as a substitute for proper therapeutic intervention. There are many different types of anxiety including; Panic Attacks, Social Anxiety, Generalised Anxiety Disorder, Obsessive Compulsive Disorder, Specific Phobias and Post

Traumatic Stress Disorder. Although the general principles are the same, they all have different treatment protocols within CBT. For example the treatment for Obsessive Compulsive Disorder is based around Exposure and Response Prevention (ERP) whereas the treatment for Post Traumatic Stress Disorder is more about helping the brain to process previously unprocessed memories and help it realise that the threat is not happening 'here and now' (usually experienced in the form of flashbacks), but actually happened in the past and are no longer a threat. If you do believe that you may be suffering from a clinical level of anxiety that is impacting on your life, I hope that this short section on anxiety has helped you to decide that it would be worthwhile to seek out professional help.

Epilogue

So, we have officially reached the physical end of the book. If it is your first time of reading it through then you have possibly not tried any, or all, of the practical exercises. But you probably know what I am going to say next. That's right; Go and get a planning diary and write in a time and date when you will start to go through the book a second time, but this will be when you actually work through it with pen and paper at hand. If this is your second time through you should now have a much better idea of what you are going to do with your one and only life and how you are going to get there. I am sure that you will need to refer back to different sections of the book as you start to turn your journey and destination into reality. Don't plan too many weeks ahead as you work through the book and make sure that you are comfortable with each stage before you move ahead. However, that shouldn't stop you adding other things into your planning diary right now if they are aligned with you starting to live a more congruent life.

We have covered a lot of techniques and methods in this book. It is possible that many, if not all, of them are quite new to you. You now have a tool box full of pretty much everything you need to figure out what you want to do with your life, and then set off on the journey towards getting it. As with the tools we use for other things we do in our lives, the trick is to practice with them and start to master them. This is important; you should be the master of the tools you are using, not the other way round.

The other thing you now have is an overall framework. Have a look at the diagram in the summary to Part One. That will show you where you are on the journey and give you a view on where to go next. Many examples have been given in this book as to the sort of directions many people might want to take their lives. But yours might not be amongst them. So, many apologies to anyone who wants to; be an opera singer, a circus acrobat, a film director, a racing driver, a stand up comedian, or a laboratory technician. The principles still apply to all of these and more. And what you choose to do with your one life might have nothing to do with a particular future career path or major project. You might simply find that you have just drifted slightly off track and only slight adjustments are needed to get back on course. Only you can decide what is congruent and important for you.

As I mentioned at the end of Part One, if you have found the ideas in this book useful, please do leave a short summary or comment in the review section on Amazon. I would love to know if you have moved from being a small origami boat drifting down a stream and have become a sturdy rowing boat with full control over where you are going. – Of course you could also imagine yourself as being a powerful sailboat being skilfully piloted and mastering any weather or tides that nature throws your way as you chart your own course and destination. You have possibly guessed that this is the metaphor I like to use. Metaphors can be very powerful tools - have a go at thinking one up that best fits you.

All the very best to you.
Paul Green

CPSIA information can be obtained
at www.ICGtesting.com
Printed in the USA
LVHW112307101218
600001LV00001B/212/P